A Deficient Purist

A Deficient Purist

Stories of hunting, fishing, dogs, and friends

by

Kevin Kennedy

What others are saying about *A Deficient Purist*

Whenever we receive a submission from Kevin Kennedy, I set time aside to enjoy what I know will be a well-told adventure that reminds me of a similar experience of my own. He is equally capable of sparking fond memories from years ago or reflecting upon a hunting or fishing trip that happened only yesterday, always with a keen observational wit that leaves me looking forward to more.
—Mike Floyd, Editor, *Gray's Sporting Journal*

Kevin Kennedy admits it right up front: He doesn't want his "outdoor adventures to be bland, beige, boring, or devoid of uncertainty." They're not. He's the guy with the leaky boat and broken ribs whose hunting and fishing stories make you nod your head and laugh. He's been there, it's what he loves.
—Eileen Clarke, author *The Queen of The Legal Tender Saloon* and a dozen wild game cookbooks.

For my family and decades of dogs.
Both have immeasurably enhanced everything.

I've led a life chock-full of stories, and I know now that you have to be shifty and vigilant and ready to receive their incoming fire. Sometimes it takes the passage of years to reveal their actual meaning or import.

Pat Conroy

Table of Contents

Introduction

With the publication of this wide-ranging collection of stories and essays, Kevin Kennedy's sure-footed prose should get more of the attention that it deserves.

Years ago, writer John Barsness posited that hunters and anglers could be divided into specialists and generalists, the former becoming experts in one outdoor niche while the latter are content to remain journeymen while enjoying the wide variety of activities available in the outdoors. Kennedy is definitely a generalist (as am I), and this book can be seen as a celebration of that choice.

The result is a delightful smorgasbord: big game with both rifles and bows; upland birds and waterfowl; settings ranging from the American West to Africa and the Sea of Cortez. When discussing the collection early on, I pointed out that a lot of work in this genre successfully focuses on one theme related by geography, quarry, or equipment and technique, and one could argue in favor of that approach. Fortunately, Kevin had the good sense to ignore that suggestion, and I'm glad he did.

A short, random sample illustrates the point. "A Deficient Purist" explores the contrast between fishing with fly rods and conventional tackle without ever becoming judgmental. "A Fitting Introduction?" describes the satisfaction of introducing beginners to the outdoors while laughing over some families' occasional resentment of the resulting time away from home. "Thursday Buck" combines a strong sense of family (Kevin's two sons) with a spot-on feel for the Eastern Montana prairie. "Comes a Kudu" conveys the excitement of a first African bow-hunt without ever lapsing into cliché. In none of these pieces does the author attempt to inflate his abilities or claim expertise he does or does not have (although in fact he usually does).

Although it may not seem apparent upon first glance, common themes do unite these pieces, although they are not the usual ones referenced earlier. Instead, we find respect for friends, love of family, and appreciation of wild places no matter what is (or is not) shot or caught. Accomplishments are savored rather than trumpeted, and nature itself assumes the role of leading character. All this adds up to just the kind of thoughtful writing the outdoor genre should see more often.

Don Thomas
Lewistown, Montana

Author's Note

This collection of essays celebrates the excitement, challenge, mishaps, friendships, human and canine, occasional angst, and the pure fun of hunting, fishing, and being outdoors. I have been doing these things for a long time and I'm aware that I, like most of us, am not elite, but joyously stumble through these endeavors.

My intent with these tales, is to engage and entertain. Like an ongoing conversation between old friends on a long pickup ride to a place stiff with birds, fish, deer, or just the enticing buzz of potential. I hope to bring an occasional grin, a hint of nostalgia and recognition, and to fire up the imaginations of those early in their hunting and angling adventures, as the storytellers in books and magazines of my youth did, and still do, for me.

While compiling these thoughts I relived some amazing moments. I smelled sage, pine, and elk. I felt the downhill speed and rumble of rapids under my canoe, the weight of meat laden packs, and the absolute rush of puckering proximity to large wild animals. I spent time again with dogs and buddies I miss, and walked or waded places that "progress" and a volcano altered forever.

I think you'll find that you and I have covered some of the same, or at least adjacent ground. If any of these stories provide a glimpse behind the curtain to an uninitiated friend or family member, so much the better. Those of us whose best days are spent outdoors are sometimes a conundrum to our friends and families. Our passions bewildering, our penchant for long, often arduous, days afield, a puzzle to them, yet compulsory for us.

All of these stories, save one, are as accurate as my memories can make them. Even the one fiction piece, Dreamember, is "true" though generously garnished with literary license and imagination.

Another of these stories shares its title with this book.

The concept of *A Deficient Purist* is the general theme running through these essays. I'm competent…to a degree, certainly experienced, and definitely passionate. I have been privileged to observe, learn from, and share campfires, night skies, capsized canoes, excruciating heat, blizzards, amazing sights and unforgettable days with many whose expertise and standards eclipse my own.

I recognize and acknowledge the difference.

Like a lot of hunters and anglers, I have mental images of my heroic prowess in the wilderness. I am a shining example of manly competence as I star in my memories and fantasies, but, in real life, events don't always unwind as I envision.

In this collection, I attempt to convey some of the anticipation and optimism required to dive into venues and activities with enthusiasm and to see them through to their uncertain, usually rewarding, and occasionally surprising outcomes.

Bowhunting, bird hunting with dogs, fishing, rifle hunting, interactions with interesting characters, and time spent on the water are all represented but are rarely the topic. Each adventure provides a setting. The stories wander.

Nothing in these pages will enhance your skill with a rod, rifle, bow, or shotgun but I hope you might smile, be prodded to make plans, nod at a memory, or possibly blink away a sudden mistiness.

Thank you for sharing these days with me.

Kev

Prelude

It must have been the magazine ads that got me. I had never shot a real bow, and I knew no one who hunted with or even owned a bow, but I knew I needed one with the soul deep certainty that a goose knows to head South in the fall. I had no choice.

I got my first recurve when I was fourteen. It was 62 inches of beautiful. I loved everything about it—its color, the feel of the grip. Even the name, Wing Falcon, implied speed and grace.

Chuck at Ye Olde Archery Shoppe had my Falcon hanging, among less comely bows, on the rack behind the cash register with a sticker that read $42.00. With tax the cost soared to over $44.00. Add in three fiberglass arrows, because everyone needs some "good" arrows, then three more wood arrows for practice, and it seemed like I was always going to be about ten lawns from being able to afford it.

My buddy Bruce had his eye on a bow, too. Looking at us, Chuck could see our angst, or possibly he foresaw a long and profitable relationship. Either way, he set us up with a time payment plan. We couldn't take the bows with us until they were paid in full, but we could shoot for free in his basement range. It was a three-mile bike ride each way from my house to Chuck's shop, but it was worth it to spend spring Saturdays and early summer shooting and just handling that graceful, sensuous piece of art.

When I finally handed Chuck the last five-dollar bill to pay off that bow, I shot a lot. I had read that shooting at small targets was important, so Bruce and I shot at dandelions, matchbooks, and bottle caps scattered around the lawn. We scoffed at the occasional archery article with pictures of well-dressed people shooting at 3-foot round, multicolored straw targets on easels. We shot from the garage roof or kneeling under my mom's rhododendron. The ad people were always on a lawn. Weenies!

We had constant bruises on our arms and hard calluses on our fingers because we wouldn't waste our arrow money on armguards or tabs, but we were good. I have probably never shot as well as I did in those days.

My bow always had a faint lemony smell because if I wasn't shooting, I felt that a committed archer like me should get the Pledge, a rag, and polish my bow.

Daily, we shot in our yards, but frequently we'd go to the Tracks. It was close enough to ride our bikes in a half hour. "The Tracks" was a railroad right-of-way with pastures, swamps, and a few acres of woods. It ran from 72nd all the way to 84th street, but on each end the last couple hundred yards was pretty tame and had barking dogs.

For a couple of boys living in town it was a portal to the wild. Our wilderness, like our targets, was small, but it was real. There was the possibility of rabbits. We sometimes found coon tracks. We got to know the look and sound of different hawks, found a snag where a screech owl lived, and once we argued for a week over whether that little almost robin looking bird was a Rufus Sided Towhee, or Rufus Sighted Towhee, red eyes adding to the confusion. Another bike ride, this one to the Fern Hill Library, settled that debate.

I shot my first big game at the Tracks, a bullfrog. Frog legs frying in a blackened mess kit fry pan over a backyard fire might as well have been Dall sheep ribs on a Brooks Range mountainside, and maybe the best thing I'd ever eaten.

Once I fell off my bike on the way to the Tracks. I don't recall what happened to cause the crash, but I do remember putting a nick in the finish of my bow, the huge gash as I called it at the time. That bow was made of wood and magic and, along with my bike, it transported me from my normal neighborhood to the wilds of the Yukon. Now I'd ruined it.

Surprisingly, despite the wound, it shot as well as ever, so the pain I suffered from doing injury to my bow faded over the summer into early fall. It was still beautiful, but now it was more a hunter's bow—it had history, character.

That December, an amazing thing happened. Bruce and I asked our parents to let us go hunting during Christmas break.

They said OKAY.

No kid who ever asked for a car, a trip to Disneyland, or a horse and were granted their wish, was ever more surprised or excited.

My dad agreed to drop me and Bruce in a meadow about an hour south of town along with camping gear, canned chili, and our bows. Bruce's dad would pick us up three whole days later.

Fred Bear had nothing on us.

I'd hunted deer before but never two consecutive days… and never with a bow. My hunting partners, my dad and my uncles, hunted three days a year. The deer season was two weeks long. With work six days a week, the math was easy. I started going one day a year when I turned nine and all three days at twelve. By fourteen, I'd carried a rifle for two years but had never seen a legal buck and few does.

Bruce had never actually hunted deer, but he worked part-time after school at a taxidermy shop. This gave him an aura of expertise that rivaled and some days exceeded my six days of carrying a bolt action 30-30 around Olympic Peninsula clearcuts.

This trip, though, was taking things to a new level.

Not only were we going camping, in December, by ourselves, but we'd be bowhunting deer! Despite only having seen a handful of bucks in my life and none during a hunting season, visions of giant blacktail bucks nearly overwhelmed me. There were few designated bow seasons in those days, but the archery regs allowed hunters to shoot does. Bruce and I very seriously discussed our plan to pass all kinds of bucks and settle for a spike or a "meat doe" on the last day if the right buck didn't show. "Would a 2-point do on the second day or was that a morning of the third day buck?" The anticipation was delicious.

Despite Bruce's tenure at the taxidermy shop, I had not only killed that bullfrog with my bow but I had once shot a rabbit with a .22. I was pretty certain my experience would trump Bruce's ability to judge trophy quality. Bruce pointed out that I had failed 100% of the time while deer hunting so far, and he would surely have two mounts in his room if he'd had all the chances to hunt that I did.

The stakes were high. I didn't know if I could survive if Bruce got a bigger buck than me on this trip.

It was a wonderful first deer camp. We cooked meals on a Coleman stove. We splashed around trying to grab splotchy, toothy, rotting, spawning Coho salmon from a creek. We walked logging roads in the dark hoping to hear a coyote or an owl, and, though neither would ever admit it, to confront our unspoken fear of the woods at night.

Our tent collapsed one night due to rain and wind, requiring us to set it back up and run lines to nearby trees to shore up the flimsy, and now broken, aluminum frame. When we climbed back into our sleeping bags with the tent ugly but standing, we felt as proud and competent as though we'd designed and built a suspension bridge.

We were cold, wet, sometimes scared, and completely exhilarated.

On the last morning, I saw a deer.

It was a doe, maybe even a fawn of the year, but it was a deer and that was why I was there. Everything about the minimum-sized buck we'd take had evaporated before my dad had driven away three days before.

She was close, easily within range, but with no gap to thread an arrow between the crosshatch of alder and naked vine maples. She knew something or someone was nearby. She was nervous. I had an arrow nocked, and my fingers were tight on the string as we shared that brush patch. Her ears flicked around as she tried to figure out why she was uneasy, and I fought to control my tremors.

I have no idea how long I got to be with that deer, but I owe her. The awakening of the ancient in me took place in that Pierce County tree farm. I never drew my bow before she took a few steps, further obscuring my view, then raised her tail and bounded away. I could hear her long after she was out of sight.

Bruce wouldn't believe me at first. I had to swear on my dog Nikki that I'd seen a deer.

When Bruce's dad arrived that afternoon to take us home, it was just days before Christmas. Nothing under the tree would compare with what we'd found in our first deer camp.

Someday we'd come home with meat and antlers as well as stories, but for now we knew we had crossed a line that we'd never uncross.

We couldn't drive, didn't shave, and were just beginning to realize that girls were more interesting than we'd previously thought, but we'd connected with the past and our own innate nature.

We weren't yet men, but we were hunters.

Getting 'em Out

"Ri, I got a bull, a big one."

I knew I sounded pretty calm, but it had been a heck of a morning. The hours between when I first laid hands on the moose and access to a phone had been enough time for me to calm down and consider my situation.

I had a bull moose lying a thousand yards up a steep soggy hillside above a landing at the end of an old logging road. That landing was a legit three miles from a gate that prohibited driving any closer.

Three miles is not that far. It's about an hour walk on flat ground, or a leisurely ninety-minute huckleberry-picking saunter. However, the prospect of moving a horse-sized carcass that far is an attention grabber of the highest order.

Due to good planning, and a little luck, nineteen years before, my wife gave birth to our twin sons, Jake and Riley. After years of playing high school football and lifting weights, they were both attending the same university about a three-hour drive from where my moose lay.

I continued on my call, "Get Jake, your boots, and your backpacks and let's haul a moose off a mountain."

I gave him directions, gathered a sack of knives and sharpeners, and headed back to the moose.

I had a lot of the blade work completed when the guys arrived. With me on the knives, combined with their youth and stamina, we got most of the moose to the landing late that night. Jake and Riley headed back to campus, and I went to bed. The next morning, a friend with horses joined me to complete the hauling. By early afternoon, I was in my pickup full of meat and antlers, headed for home.

Preparation is a key to moving meat. Strong sons and friends with horses are two critical components of that preparation.

Sometimes, however, circumstances dictate that one must rely on less ideal methods of transport.

Hefting a load on to your back is the standard. This can range from grabbing a turkey by the feet, then slinging him over a shoulder, to struggling under a compressed load of boned out meat that rivals the weight of the packer.

A word on weight: a number of years ago, the Washington Department of Game (it's called Fish and Wildlife now) published a report on the mountain goat harvest. Sex, horn length, and weight were reported. Most reports were for mature goats with 8–9-inch horns. Both billies and nannies were consistently around 300 lbs. One goat was listed at only 143 lbs. and had an asterisk next to the weight. The footnote explained that the 143-pounder was weighed on a scale. The others were estimated weights.

I understand those goat hunters. I have experienced the disappointment that comes from weighing a pack and finding it to be a lot lighter than I'd thought. It's like a fall that leaves you with terrible pain and a limp but no bruise or blood to indicate what a tough guy you must be to soldier on.

I've learned a basic weight lesson, then foolishly relearned it several times. That lesson is, there is no prize for carrying too much.

I weighed a pack one time. With my gear and a big chunk of mule deer, it weighed 130 lbs. (estimated weight well over 200 lbs.). From where that buck fell to the nearest vehicle access was certainly under a mile, but it was all uphill, and it was hot. Not take off my hat hot, or unzip my sweater hot, but desert mountains of Eastern Oregon, mid-August, no shade hot. In retrospect, it would have saved time and been infinitely easier on my body to make two trips.

That day was what is now called a teaching moment. I was worn out and dehydrated. While that was not my first triple digit pack, it was my heaviest, and my last.

You don't need a backpack to over carry. On a trip to British Columbia, my buddy Bruce shot a beautiful, honey-colored black bear. He was determined to carry it the quarter mile to a road on his shoulders.

It was a good bear but not huge. Gutted, so I guessed a net of maybe 150 lbs. Between the bear and the truck was low brush and some logging leftovers, but mostly flat, so, for that distance, it was doable. There were three of us on that trip. Stu and I, standing in back of Bruce, hoisted the bear and lightly tossed it onto his shoulders. I think if Bruce hadn't ducked a bit, our gentle toss would have been perfect. As it turned out, Bruce's head slipped into the body cavity. He had sort of a bear hat—no, more than that; it was a warm, sticky hoody.

He spoke up right away. It was hard to understand exactly what he was saying, his words muffled by the ribcage, but his tone was clear, and somewhat urgent. He wanted his head out of the bear. He sank to his knees where Stu and I were able to peel the bear off. Seeing Bruce emerge from that bear, his face bloody and being stretched by the bear's flank, was weirdly reminiscent of watching my kids being born.

On the next toss, we nailed it.

Non-hunters, even experienced hunters with dozens of woodlot whitetails to their credit, don't quite understand the logistical issues that arise when getting a large animal home from the hills.

Heavy loads that flop are hard to handle.

I was entertaining my wife once with the story of how Jack and I took multiple trips to get a Roosevelt bull from the bottom of a canyon up to a gated road where we were able to reach it with horses.

"The bull was right in the bottom of a cut in the bottom of a canyon, probably 800 yards below the road—"

"Eight hundred yards, that's not very far," she pointed out. "Shouldn't have taken you very long at all."

"But…uh," I sputtered, "it's not like walking around a track. It was raining and muddy and steep. In fact, it was so steep, we were on all fours, grabbing handfuls of mud, and still we'd slide back a foot for every two feet we'd climb. It was—"

"Still, not very far."

"Yeah, well, what if I said you needed to get your car up a telephone pole?" I had her now. "What about that? That's not very far either, huh, is it?"

"That's stupid," she said, and I was dismissed.

But sometimes getting meat out can seem as hard as putting a car up a pole.

Most hunters I know have done the classic deer on a pole carry. A pole 3 inches thick and 8–10 feet long is perfect. The front legs of the deer are lashed together around the ankles and the rear legs snugged to each other as well. Then the pole is slid between the legs. Two hunters each grab an end of the pole and they're off, the deer hanging neatly between them. Usually, it only takes a few steps to realize the head must be dealt with. A few minutes of lashing the antlers between the front legs and they're off again, striding out. That's when the swinging starts. Even a modest size deer when it gets a good rhythm can pound the pole into your shoulder with the force of John Henry driving railroad spikes.

The best time to use the pole carry is for a quick photo. A couple of hero shots, then abandon the pole and either carve the deer into packable sized pieces or drag it.

The pole carry is akin to eating Mergansers. Everyone needs to try it once, if only to understand how bad it really is.

Speaking of Mergansers, rivers can be a big help in moving meat. I have personally never carried game any larger than ducks or fish in a canoe or kayak, but a friend of mine frequently hauls moose from the hinterlands of his guide area down a river. He's able to float to a spot where he can get his truck within a few feet of his freighter canoe. That may be the best moose moving method ever.

A friend and I once drifted an Alaskan river. My partner shot bull caribou on that trip, and we floated over 100 miles in a raft. Even though to get home we had three different planes and a truck ride in front of us, when we got that bull from where he fell on the tundra to the raft, it felt as though we'd completed the mission.

To me, getting meat "out" means getting it to some sort of motorized, or at least not human powered, transport.

Hauling meat is really the marrow of the hunt. It's the one thing that truly defines what is really going on. Driving an ATV to a kill site is great. If I had an ATV and could get it to where I had an elk on the ground, I know I'd do it, and be thankful for the convenience.

But I remember, and cherish, the memories of those tougher packs.

Hiking across the Tundra at sun-up to retrieve the last load of my partner's caribou and finding the boned meat still cached but the backbone, ribcage, hips, and pelvic bones gone added a flavor to that trip that couldn't have been duplicated by driving to and away from that spot. That was another teaching moment. While looking over my shoulder for the fiftieth time, I decided right there to never again spend time around a gut pile in grizzly country armed with nothing more formidable than my recurve bow.

I look at the moose rack on my kitchen wall and remember my sons by my side packing meat down a midnight mountain. We kept our flashlights off to preserve our night vision. Near the bottom, I stumbled and fell under my heavy load. Looking up, I could clearly see the silhouette of my son, the antlers over his shoulders black against the Milky Way, asking me, "You just going to lie there?"

I didn't just lie there. I awkwardly but eventually reacquired a feet-on-the-ground posture. Nearby we stashed the moose meat. The three of us, feeling light and almost giddy without our packs, walked under the stars on the gated road out to our trucks and headed respectively to campus and camp. After all, they had classes to attend, and I needed some rest. I had to be back in the morning…with a friend who has horses.

A Deficient Purist

"…and I'm telling you, those grizzly tracks were so fresh, water was just beginning to seep into them. The bank was littered with partially eaten salmon, and the river was too deep to wade and too cold to swim. The only way to continue was a trail into thick brush, almost a tunnel—the same path the bear tracks went. So, we left that fishing hole to the griz and headed back downstream."

We talked a little more about egg patterns for trout during a sockeye run and other good fish in pretty places. When our empty glasses needed attention, my new friend and I parted with a promise to talk again.

I often end up talking hunting or fishing at social events. If I had input in creating the guest list, at least a couple of my like-minded cronies will be in attendance. More often though, I'm an intriguing anomaly. I'm able to look like I belong, but they know.

I can do my part in a conversation about theater, music, travel, the night sky, American literature, active versus passive money management, or whether Australopithecus was really bipedal, but those topics rarely come up. People approach me about fly fishing.

Ever since young Brad Pitt lost his footing in that Montana river in the movie of Maclean's *A River Runs Through It*, it's as though "fishing" and "fisherman" have been erased from the lexicon and been replaced with "flyfishing" and the androgenous "fisher."

I am a fly fisherman, or fisher, but I'm not defined by that. Flyfishing and I have been together a long time. We have a great relationship, but we're not exclusive…it's complicated.

I like to be where fish live. I like to catch fish. When I feel the thump of a revived steelhead kicking out of my hands to rejoin the current, whether the hook I remove is below a metal blade or delicately wrapped in hair and feathers means less to me than the fish, the setting, and my companions.

There are even days when fish I catch run a significant risk of ending up filleted rather than nursing a sore lip.

I had a great day of fishing last fall, one of my best ever. I lost track of the number of steelhead I caught! I've had decades that didn't match the total hook ups that day.

I caught more fish than Dave!

Dave is an elite angler. If you took him to your home water, he'd take a break after each fish to savor the moment, yet still outfish you 3 to 1. He hasn't caught a fish on anything other than a fly rod in the twenty some years I've known him.

Part of that magical steelhead day we were using identical terminal tackle: a small pink jig with a trailing, bead-adorned hook below. All beneath a "strike indicator"—a floating object heathens like me call a bobber.

Dave, casting from the front of the raft, elegantly presented this setup to the fish with a fly rod, while I stood in back of our guide Phil's position at the oars. I was flinging the same offering with a spinning rod and an open-faced reel.

Phil and Dave are fly fishers. They are also gentlemen. They shared my pleasure with each fish but would not fish as I did. Late in the day, the urgency of our casting and catching cooled while our telling of tales warmed up. Drifting toward the takeout, basking in golden October afternoon sun and my rare upset over the favored steelhead, I realized that Dave felt a little…it wasn't guilt, more a recognition, at least to him, that we'd had a bit more advantage than we deserved, as though the refs liked us. The close calls went our way.

Phil and Dave drop the names of legendary steelhead rivers, even specific drifts on those rivers, as casually as my granddaughter drops cheerios on her highchair tray. In conversation that day, I learned that the way we were fishing, though perfectly legal, might provoke a fist fight on some of British Columbia's steelhead water. Some consecrated fly fishers would consider our methods as akin to being caught with a Folgers can full of nightcrawlers. The beauty of the canyon, the dramatic fall colors, and the ferocity of the fish on this once in a lifetime day earned a permanent spot on my mental highlight reel. Dave switched to swinging a fly two fish into the morning, but I could tell he regretted waiting even that little while.

I first encountered this focus on style in the form of an eight-year-old boy. I was a teenager myself. We were hunting black bears with a mixed pack of Blueticks, Walkers, and Plotts. The dogs were running a hot track, and we'd split up. Al, a mentor of mine, as well as the guy who owned the dogs, was following the hounds on foot while I had his son with me in my truck. The boy and I cruised the labyrinth of logging roads trying to reacquire the faint bugling of the hounds after we'd lost them over a ridge. The two of us pulled up to listen at landing near the top of a clearcut. We didn't hear the dogs, but I spotted a bear, a different bear, grazing several hundred yards below us in the cut.

I grabbed the old Savage .30-30 from the rack in the back window of my beat-up blue Chevy pickup intent on collecting my first bear rug. I was jacked!

The kid, watching me, incredulous, said, "What are you doing?"

"I'm going after that bear." The *duh* was implied.

"You can't shoot a bear the dogs didn't chase. That ain't right."

I stared at the little wet blanket for a moment, may or may not have said something inappropriate, and told him to wait right there while I went bear hunting.

The bear fed off into the timber never knowing I was stalking him. It was too late anyway. That little…the kid…had drained my enthusiasm and set me to wondering what kind of a sorry hound man I was. Was I someone who would sneak up on a bear that hadn't even been treed?

That adherence to a standard—whether style, size, or manner—can be admirable. Without self-imposed rules, it's unlikely one would ever reach elite status. But the bear snob was eight!

I get it, though. Occasionally, through the campfire smoke and mist, I glimpse the heart of the purist. I once spent ten days in Alaska frequently and fruitlessly creeping within about three times my effective range of bull caribou.

I wanted a caribou bad. I'd dreamed of those exotic antlers and clicking hooves since I was a kid, and there they were, within easy rifle range, but I was packing my recurve bow. My partner offered his rifle, and though I confess, I did briefly consider it, I was surprised how easy it was to ultimately turn it down. I went to Alaska not to kill a caribou, but to kill a caribou with my bow. I ended that trip with neither a caribou nor a regret.

Conversely, a few years after that, I drew a once-in-a-lifetime bull moose permit in my home state of Washington. I hunted a week with my bow. I passed a point-blank chance on a yearling bull but never got close to a grown-up moose. I went home from that early season hunt mooseless. When I returned a couple weeks later with my rifle, I hung my tag on a terrific Shiras bull. I have no ambivalence about that bull or the hunt. I never felt as though I'd settled or sold out. I had two excellent hunts with that one tag.

So, what spark do purists have that I lack? What refinement, extra bit of sophistication, or gene do they possess where I'm lacking?

My friend Dwight, an unambiguous purist, calls me a dilettante. He means it derisively, but I've always responded to his jab with gratitude. I explained that I consider it a synonym for Renaissance Man.

Dwight, by every measure, is a better bowhunter than me. He's more dedicated, he's absurdly fit, and he's still hunting just as hard at dusk on the last day of a ten-day hunt as he did the first morning.

I'm jealous of what he's done and is doing still. But Dwight has never caught a marlin or a rooster fish on a fly or bait. He has never shared his life or his home with a bird dog.

I envy Dave's abilities with a fly rod, one- or two-handed. His casts are precise, stylish, and effective. His knowledge of fish and flies, encyclopedic. From my experience fishing with him, it's inevitable that he'll hook more and bigger fish than is reasonable, certainly more and bigger fish than me.

Dave is such a dedicated fly fisherman that he gave me and my sons his shotguns.

I'm humbled when confronted with such focus.

I'm humbled and impressed, but not envious. Okay, a little envious. I'm reminded of a quote from a long-ago sitcom where two perfectly fine-looking women see a stunning model type strut by their sidewalk café table. They watch her pass. As she disappears down the block, one remarks to the other, "I'd do literally anything to have a body like that…except, of course, diet and exercise."

The purists among us, like great beauties and star athletes, show us what is achievable. It's a standard that many of us have the potential to, if not meet, at least approach. Even when we fall short, we have the capacity to improve substantially. Ay, there's the rub. The opportunity cost of excellence rather than mere, possibly near, competence is too great for me.

I've come to accept my status as a dilettante/Renascence Man. I embrace my scattered focus and my undistinguished capabilities in the field.

To the purist, I may appear devoted to mediocrity, a pillar of average, but I see my spinning gear and my fly rod, my rifle and my bow, my dog, my canoe, and my side-by-side 20 as magic carpets that fly me to spectacular and surprising destinations. Abandoning any would create an unacceptable void.

I've caught fish and immersed myself in fishy places I know would delight Dwight. Dave might want his shotguns back if he shared just one more morning with me on a tilted desert mountainside, absorbing the expansive sunrise while listening to chukar talk. I know, though, that both will continue to be enraptured with and committed to their passions while I remain just outside the sanctified realm of the purist.

But I have an all-access pass.

When sharing a campfire with the best bowhunters, I understand them in a way only another bowhunter can. While not exactly a peer, what they've done a thousand times, I've done a hundred. I know false summits, blown opportunities, and the mélange of emotion and hyper focus that cannot be explained to a bowhunting virgin when a bull elk screams his dominance while close enough to count his eyelashes.

My fish stories don't always include a flyrod and never begin with me calculating the best fly to match the hatch. I tie on what Dave tells me. But as steelhead and salmon with my sons, tarpon with my wife, or roosterfish with my daughter swim through my memory, I rarely consider the method of catch but clearly remember the smiles, the days.

So, when I'm asked about being a flyfisher, I smile, mentally sort through some appropriate stories, and begin… "Yeah, I do some fly fishing, but…"

River Reunion

Curley told me we'd catch a steelhead, and we did. Like that first steelie, I was hooked.

That was a long time ago in water that has changed more than most.

Anyone who has fished for a while has experienced the frustration of seeing homes, vacation cabins, and no trespassing signs sprout along favorite drifts on our rivers, or seeing the ugly rutted two track access road that required 4wd, sometimes even a come-along, get paved—then become a favorite of the motorhome and silver trailer set. When that happens to the places we love, we're saddened, but we adjust. Maybe move upstream a bit farther.

One sunny late Spring Sunday, the home waters of my youth mutated, in minutes, from a cool, green-hued sanctuary into a fiery hell of superheated mud and ripped up trees travelling at freeway speeds over my steelhead memories—reorganizing the landscape and wiping out every living thing in its path, including dozens of people.

The eruption of Mount St. Helens in May of 1980 ended my steelhead fishing for a long time.

As a young man, I had work, then, before long, kids, and frankly I didn't know where to go or really, very much about how to fish for steelhead.

Experience, and Curley, had shown me that if I waded and threw my #2 brass Mepps enough times, the Toutle and its tributaries would give me steelhead in August and September. But the Toutle and those alluring feeder streams were gone. I didn't know other rivers. The holes, drifts, the personalities of those rivers and their steelhead were other angler's secrets. Besides, I was busy.

Turned out "busy" was cover. Sure, I had stuff to do, but in retrospect I was in mourning. My river had died. Its death was violent and unexpected. I grieved and moved on.

There was plenty to do. I canoed smallmouth waters. I rafted big rivers, caught other kinds of fish and, once in a while, fondly reminisced about wading for small water steel.

I clearly recall where I was the moment I started back. I don't remember the year, but I know the spot. I was Eastbound on I-90 rolling downhill toward Missoula from Lookout Pass. A stream runs alongside the highway. Periodically it flashed me. It shook me to my core, like a teenager on the receiving end of direct eye contact and an intriguing smile from an appealing girl. Suppressed memories and feelings flooded in. I may have been in the perfect mood, or maybe it was the just right angle of afternoon sunlight on the water, but a glimpse of a deep green eddy or the riffles where a chute curved around boulder hit hard. Before I reached St. Regis, I knew it wouldn't be long before I'd be back in cut-offs and tennis shoes wading a river.

I had caught a few steelhead since the mountain blew, but they were with a guide from a boat.

I was eager to get back into a river with a spinning rod and my favorite shiny brass spinner.

I picked a river within a couple hours of my Puyallup home. I'd never fished it, but I had read it had a small summer run, and I didn't expect a crowd.

My son Riley joined me for this re-immersion.

As we got closer to the river and farther from I-5, the stars pulsed brighter before the July sunrise erased them.

We geared up just like the old days. No lightweight waders or perfectly balanced fly rods here. My frayed denim cut-offs and Converse All Stars had morphed into cargo shorts and felt-soled wading shoes, but other than that, just an old work shirt and the most pure fishing gear I've ever had: a spinning rod, wearing an open face reel stuffed with six-pound mono. A tiny brass swivel, a half a dozen spinners with a few more swivels stuffed in a pill bottle in my pocket, and I was set.

Ri and I fished upstream from the last bridge. Fewer fish lived here than down river, but I hoped it would be unlikely that we'd see another person.

It worked out just that way.

I'd done a reasonable job of getting my three kids into a lot of good situations. They all knew how to paddle rapids in both canoes and kayaks. They had experienced big white water in rafts; spent a lot of time in proximity to bears, deer, and elk; and had caught lots of fish, though none had yet known a steelhead.

The river we'd chosen had the right look. I didn't know yet if it had any fish in it, but it was beautiful. Paths through the willows to the riverbank hinted at previous anglers, but all the tracks we stepped on were made by hooves.

Though the water was cold, the sun's rays were already touching some of the treetops, promising that what was icy at dawn would be welcome when the shadows climbed down the bank.

Early morning river water is bracing, but it feels terrific, up to a point. For me, that point is just below pocket level. You can stand on your tiptoes in moving water to try to avoid that last critical inch, but that's a high-risk maneuver. It's gone both ways for me. Now that I wear wading boots rather than tennis shoes, I'm less likely to slip, but I'm also older and my center of gravity has…shifted. Steve and I used to call that arm swinging, Russian folk dancing move that everyone instinctively tries just before their hat floats, the river dance.

I felt a twinge of guilt that Ri was a grown man before he spent a day wading a summer steelhead river, but I got past it quickly as we fell into the familiar rhythms of a couple fishing buddies sussing out the most likely holding spots. There was no trail. Bends, downed logs, water depth, and the angle of the bank dictated the best places to cross.

Stepping into the river felt like lopping off decades. Even though it was new water for me, it felt as though I'd been there the day before.

When the current pushed me in familiar ways, I adjusted with no conscious thought. The tip of the beaver gnawed stick I'd found to steady myself in the deeper runs found its way into perfect niches on the rocky river bottom as though guided by providence rather than my out of practice hand. When a shadow flickered across my vision, I didn't have to think about the sun's placement, I instantly looked in the right direction to see the osprey.

Ri and I moved up the river as though we'd done it a hundred times. While he'd thoroughly work a drift, I'd move past to the next promising spot. We leapfrogged several miles of river, not in silence, but with minimal conversation, each occasionally stopping to watch the other.

The rush of moving water, even when less than knee deep, confounds any effort at talking unless you're only a wading stick apart. Other sound feels unhampered, but the human voice is swallowed by rivertalk. Communication becomes nonverbal. Pointing at the brush to signify taking a track away from the water for a while or eye contact and a smile to confirm we'd both seen the mink running along the bank.

About once an hour we'd sit and take off our boots. The magical way pebbles climb over the top of wading shoes to end up inside is the excuse, but just sitting, talking a little, and listening to the river and the subliminal sounds of bees, birds, and bugs is the prize.

My river days downstream from Mt. Saint Helens often included a cessation of casting when blacktails or elk shared a stretch of water. There is something in the sound of the river, our lack of predatory posture, or maybe it's our scent being washed away and merged with the water, but deer and elk often allowed us to get close. This new river was no different. The mewling of cow elk let us know they were there, the sight of seven velvet bulls held us. Neither of us lamented the fishing time lost as herd wandered the open expanse of a gravel bar then eventually crossed and moved on.

Rivers always have the potential to surprise. One cast might bring a ferocious attack from a smolt only twice the size of the spinner, the next, the sudden stop and living weight we'd come for.

With a combination of current and anticipation, I'd driven the hook hard into the mysteries of the river bottom many times, bent the rod, then waited in vain for the head shake or run. When it finally happened, it was as though preordained.

Sunlight had abandoned the river. Ri and I were on the way downstream, lackadaisically casting to evening water we'd thoroughly flogged earlier. My spinner splashed into an eddy below a small log jam. It sank a couple beats then, as I eased it into the edge of the current, it stopped. For a pregnant instant, nothing happened, but both the fish and I knew...then he made his move. He ripped line downstream, jumped, ran back up, jumped again, then again.

For the sake of the story, I'd love to say it was an epic battle with a 30-pound steelhead, but oddly, it was better than that. It was exactly right, a straightforward match with a game, bright fish. He was solidly hooked, and it was uncomplicated water. In less time than I would have preferred, I knelt in the shallows with the fish in my hands.

Despite the years, the larger waistband in my shorts, and worn-out knees, I recaptured for a few moments how it felt to be twenty years old discovering the allure of wading the "Tout." It was perfect. I'd fished the whole day with my son, we'd not seen another person, and we caught a fish. A wonderful, strong, and shiny fish that gave me all he had then, a quick roiling of the surface as he disappeared in the darkening water.

It was full dark when we left our last wet tracks on the still warm rocks below the truck.

In the miles before we reacquired pavement, we'd already planned to return.

It was good to be home.

Chukars: A Warning

I like chukars. I like the way they look. I like the way they taste, and I love the country in which they live. But chukars are different from quail, pheasants, and other gentlemanly birds. Chukars will try to kill you…and your dog.

Seems fair, but it does change the nature of the game a bit.

Chukar habitat makes you squint. If it's not overwhelmingly bright, there's a gritty wind. Usually, it's both. The range is big, and always tilted. I have found chukars on level ground, but invariably after climbing to a flat at the top of a ridge.

Most people don't think of bird hunting as adventure. Most people haven't hunted chukars. They're the upland equivalent of the cartoon roadrunner, and I often feel like Wile E. Coyote.

There aren't a lot of roads in good chukar country. There shouldn't be. There are no farms, no timber to cut, and in general, no reason for anyone other than hunters or hermits to be there. Thus, the few roads that exist were clearly built by crazy people.

My buddy Mark and I hunted the Idaho side of Hells Canyon a few years ago. An access road was gated and required us to check out a key from a ranger station. The ranger laughed as he told us about the many "Easterners" who borrowed the key then "chickened out" and came back within an hour or so. We laughed along with him, but I could feel a little warning tickle in the reptilian core of my brain.

The road started innocuously enough. There were nice views of the river, and the road, though narrow, was hard and almost without ruts. This was certainly better than the standard road in chukar country. As the road climbed, the vegetation shrunk until it was just short grass. The road kept climbing and winding until we came around a bend to find the road, though still hard and smooth, now just felt like a skinny shelf tacked, like a dish rail, to a mountainside a thousand feet above the river.

Just the thought of meeting a truck heading down the hill had the actual physical effect of making several of my body parts involuntarily pucker.

Narrow is a variable concept. That same road with trees along the side might have been hard on the rear-view mirrors but otherwise utterly puckerless. With nothing but clear Idaho air between my perch in the passenger seat and an easy to visualize, high speed, watery death in the canyon bottom, it had a different, more vibrant feel.

There wasn't room for a skateboard to pass, but the maniacs who built this road had thoughtfully gouged a gap out of the uphill side of the cliff every mile or so to allow for traffic. Our conversation, which had been animated and constant on the pavement, had slowed soon after the gate. It stopped entirely about 500 feet above the river. It had been quiet in the cab for some time. On spotting one of the wide spots, Mark and I both spoke up, remarking on the "turnaround," and decided that the area looked pretty barren and probably didn't hold chukars anyway.

To maintain our "Westerner" cred, we had lunch before returning the key.

In addition to the magnitude of the drop and the near perpendicular slope, that road stands out in my memory not because of how bad it was, rather because of how good.

Most access roads consist primarily of sharp rocks and deep holes. A slow speed flat tire isn't life threatening, but changing a tire can be. My son Jake and I found that out. The puny factory jack on the uneven surface required the creative use of shims. When we finally got the wheel high enough to change, the axel was resting precariously on a pile of rocks that we'd wedged in with each fraction of an inch we could wrangle from the battered jack. Though it wobbled as we carefully removed the lug nuts, we managed to swap out the flat with the undersized emergency spare, which miraculously survived all the way to town.

Whether driving or walking, careening off a cliff is always a possibility when hunting chukars, but it's certainly not the only way these diabolical birds even the odds with us.

Chukars have allies.

The most reliable of these are rattlesnakes.

In a normal day of chukar hunting, there will be a number of times when exhaustion will be nearly overwhelming. Bent over, sucking air, while envisioning friends enjoying a cold beverage and watching football on TV, can interfere with your focus and test your resolve. Yet, even at times like these, the sharp rattle of a snake next to your boot can realign your thought process more quickly than you might imagine. In these circumstances, the most sluggish among us is able to execute leaps and pirouettes that would make a Prima Ballerina blush with envy.

I have personally fully committed to this snake dance on rock piles and hillsides where normally I would want at least three points of contact, and my son Riley once pulled off a brief hover.

Despite, or maybe because of, my ability to levitate and twirl at the first sound of a snake's rattle, I haven't been bitten.

It's never been really close, as far as I know. My dogs have a different story.

My first two bird dogs never suffered a bite, but it wasn't for lack of trying. I once caught Archie trying his best to excavate a snake. He was one dinner plate-sized rock from success when I hauled him away. It was awkward. The snake was buzzing non-stop within inches of Archie's face as I tried to catch a dancing, dodging Arch and pull him away while keeping my own delicate parts out of the mix.

Like a lot of snake encounters, I heard, but I didn't see that one. I didn't see the one that bit my dog Clancy last year either.

Clancy and I, along with my friend Zeb and his two dogs decided to hunt up the Columbia River. The word was there was some pretty good hunting to be had, but it was only accessible by boat.

This is another way chukars can up their odds of bagging hunters. Besides tough, steep country and venomous snakes, there are boats.

After a quiet morning of wandering some good looking but currently, due to a recent fire, chukar free country, Clancy and I made our way back to where we'd beached the boat in a protected bay. I looked out over the river and was glad we had no deadline to get back. The wind had come up. It was ugly out in the open channel. The waves were 3 feet from top to trough with the wind blowing so hard it took the tops off the waves, leaving them level as a tabletop. The spindrift simulated a rainstorm for the first 12 feet off the surface of the river.

We'd camp in the safety of the bay today, tomorrow, too, if the wind didn't let up. There was no way we'd venture into that whitecapped chaos.

When Zeb got to the boat, he hopped in, and Clancy had to move. My poor dog screamed as though he were being burned. That was when I first noticed his right leg was swollen to twice its normal size.

It only took a few minutes to sort through what had happened. Snakebite was the only explanation.

We needed to head for town.

I checked it later: the ride from our safe, protected bay to the boat launch was 13 miles.

It seemed longer.

We took a pounding. Despite my white-knuckle grip, a single gust could turn the boat 45 degrees. For fully half the distance there was no shore, just deep water against a vertical wall.

We took off our boots.

Our gear was soaked, and it took me a while to unclench my fingers from the steering wheel, but within an hour of making it to the launch, Clancy was at a veterinarian in Ellensburg being treated for his bite.

Zeb did get a chukar that day, so we won, but barely.

The most unusual chukar plot I ever faced took place several years ago with my dog Bogan.

I had been asked by a friend to take Howard, a man I had never met, hunting. He was interested in the kind of dogs our club produces (Cesky Fousek North America) and lived near me, so I was appointed ambassador.

By mid-day, I had a bird in my vest, shot over a beautiful point, and Howard had enjoyed seeing some nice dog work.

I was partway up a shallow draw heading, like always in chukar country, toward the top of the next hogback. Bogan was working back and forth across the draw about 50 yards above me when he banged into a point.

He was locked up on small patch of brush. I don't think I'd ever seen him point with more intensity.

Howard was above and to the side of the draw. I looked at him, and he nodded that he was ready if the birds came his way. I worked around so the small brush patch was between Bogan and me. I strode in, shotgun at port arms, kicking the bushes, ready for the flush.

I don't know if it's technically called a "flush" when a cougar explodes from the cover at the end of my boot, but it was easily as exhilarating. It was a big cat. He made a noise between a scream and a growl and went right for Bogan, took one shockingly fast swipe, which Bogan miraculously dodged, then backed against the brush and gazed up at me.

It was an interesting development. We looked at each other and weighed our options. He didn't seem to want to turn his back on me to burrow back into the brush nor did he want to run away—no cover and probably 20 pounds of mule deer in his belly.

Bogan, standing next to me by this time, took a tentative step toward the cat but was happy to stop on my "whoa."

As for me, I was contemplating the cougar tag in my pocket.

We stood like that, the cougar, Bogan, and I, for a long time, several minutes. I decided pretty quickly not to shoot him. Number 6 shot at 10 feet would have done the trick, but it didn't seem right. Besides, despite the clear intent of the chukars, along with this new accomplice, to kill either me or my dog, it was a pretty cool stare down, and I didn't want to end it quickly.

It did end though, in just a few minutes, just like chukar season seems to.

It starts with oppressive heat and sweat and ends with cold ears, numb fingertips, and snow, and it blows by so fast it hurts.

The dramatically changing weather, the clean beauty of their home, big toothy predators, terrifying roads and rivers, and the instantaneous rush that accompanies the maraca-like buzz of a rattler all add to the allure of these beautiful, masked immigrants.

I enjoy following my dog across a Montana flat full of pheasants, or creeping through the sagebrush flanking a stand of Russian Olive for quail. I love sharptails in the tall grass or ruffs and blues in the trees. But the extra spice is what makes chukars my favorite, and I'll keep after them for a long time… unless they get me first.

Artifact Elk

"This is NOT what I thought it was," Bill said, while reaching for another book on the overstuffed bookshelf behind his office desk, "this is way, way older."

Bill was looking at a piece of knapped obsidian I'd found while elk hunting in the Salmon River country of Idaho. A relic left by a hunter from another time.

If I had been in better shape, this conversation wouldn't have happened. When I found the artifact, I was climbing a halfway vertical game trail at around 8,000 feet. It was September hot, and I'd drug my overfed sea level body a long way from the hogback where I'd tied my horse. I was tired and winded, with a hand on the ground for support. That hunched over posture put my face close enough to notice a glint of shiny black peeking through the dust. I wiped it clean and admired the work. It seemed fat for an arrowhead and wasn't really sharp, but it was pointy and clearly someone had made it, so what else could it be?

I wondered about the guy who had lost it. Did he discard it? Had he missed a deer or elk and been unable to find it? Maybe he'd killed an elk and lost the arrowhead in the mess and excitement of his success.

However it ended up on that ridge, it went home with me.

Later that fall, I called the Department of Anthropology at Washington State University.

"Hi," I said. "While bowhunting elk, I found an obsidian point. I'll be in Pullman next week to visit my kids. I was wondering if there's someone I could show this to and talk with?"

"Well," the voice on the phone said, "I've been an anthropologist for a long time, and I specialize in stone tools of indigenes people of the Northwest. My name is Bill, but first things first, did you get an elk?"

I knew I'd found the right guy.

When I sent Bill a picture, he diagnosed my find as not an arrowhead but a dart point—a dart being the projectile flung by an atlatl, a sling-like weapon that predated bows. But later, when we met in Bill's office, things changed. My little piece of obsidian was never meant to be the tip that would pierce the hide of a deer or elk. It was the back of a spear. The part an ancient hunter had lashed to a shaft.

"This was made at least…10,000 years ago," Bill said, "maybe 12,000 years."

I felt shivers up my back as I asked, "You mean the guy that lost it might have been hunting mammoths?"

"Yeah," Bill said, throwing his arms wide, "or those great big bison!"

In the weeks that went by after Bill explained the provenance of the fractured spear, images of the prehistoric hunter kept swirling around my mind. I imagined hunting giant bison, horses, or even mammoths…with a spear!

I eventually realized that what stirred my hunter's heart was not the tiny broken tool I had found, nor the age of the artifact, or even the stunning thought of trying to somehow get a spear between the ribs of prehistoric giants. I was struck by the realization that the man who broke his spear that long ago day was not an abstraction. Not a grunting cliché caveman squatting by a fire while gnawing on a bone. He was me. He was us.

Our paths crossed at a spot near what would become the Montana/Idaho border. Though we were separated by thousands of years, we are bound by our common experience.

Sure, he would have envied our recurves and longbows with their almost magical ability to deal death from the amazing distance of 30 steps, but he had much better local knowledge.

The day I found his broken spearhead, I was hunting because I love to hunt. I love the process, and I wanted to make meat for me and my family. I imagine he enjoyed hunting, too, but the stakes were much higher for him. My unfilled tags never mean unfilled bellies. He needed success. His survival depended on it. I think the fact that he got old enough to become a competent knapper indicates he had it.

I have no doubt he was a better hunter than me. I have a good game eye, but if we were hunting together, I'll bet he'd point out animals I'd miss. He'd make me pause to listen to sounds I hadn't heard, or, having heard, hadn't interpreted. A displaced twig or the lay of the grass would probably convey meaning to him that would elude me completely.

Those differences mean little. If I lived as he did, I know I'd become aware of the subtle nuances of the natural world I now overlook. In my world, he'd easily learn to navigate traffic and work a smart phone.

Where my lug soles overlaid his footprint in the duff on that Idaho ridge is an intersection, a place where he and I and our shared experiences connect across time.

Ten thousand years ago or this fall, he and I could communicate. We would be without a common spoken language, but with the understanding of hunters.

He knew, like I do, the anticipation that makes the last few steps approaching the top of the ridge easier, followed by the head shaking frustration of a false summit. He'd sit for a moment to readjust his attitude, and then resolutely continue his climb.

Despite his skill, he failed more than he succeeded. He knew the shoulder sagging feeling of a tiny puff of breeze cooling the sweat on the back of his neck just before he reached that critical distance where he could thrust or throw his spear into the chest of his quarry, and he relived the times when he did everything right, right up to the instant he missed.

He must have had moments where he stopped to marvel at the low morning sun sparkling through water droplets on a spider web or the pattern of frost on a leaf only to turn and make eye contact with a potential meal a lance length away.

I suspect, as his target crashed off, he made a comment that you or I would clearly understand.

He would have been lost on occasion. He knew the perplexing feeling when an entire river wasn't where it was supposed to be. His brow furrowed when he'd walked twice as far as he should have and nothing looked familiar. I think he would have had a wry smile when he got his bearings, then realized that his gait was noticeably slower than it had been just moments before. He never worried about his safety, but he knew someone else did. So, he didn't stay lost as long as he would have liked.

If I don't get the shot or if I miss, I'll be okay but still, I understand and appreciate some of what he felt.

I know the instant certainty of a well-placed arrow…or spear, and the growing anxiety that creeps in within the next few heartbeats. We've shared the momentary tension when a blood trail abruptly stops and the deep satisfaction of picking it up again minutes and yards away. And we both know how it feels when the trail ends as it should, creeping in for final confirmation and finally touching, claiming our prize.

Causing the death of a large animal probably didn't allow him the mixed feelings that we have the luxury to indulge today. It would mean elation and relief. It was not only the attainment of a goal, but critical food for many; a hide, maybe horns, tusks, claws, or antlers for tools or talismans and, like today, the kill was likely accompanied by an element of awe and gratitude.

For sure it meant hard work.

Alone, wrestling a carcass many times his size and breaking it down with a stone knife, he would try to ignore the bees and insects that accompanied a warm weather kill, and in winter the heat emanating from the carcass as he worked would keep his fingers from becoming clumsy with the cold.

He knew the pleasure and pain of hauling meat and the stoicism required to pick up a heavy pack again after a needed break. He'd sigh upon reaching camp after a long haul, lay down almost more than he could carry, then take a deep breath and head back for the next load.

We would not need words to share the relief, the utter joy of getting the last of the meat and hide out of a canyon and back to the truck, or to the communal fire.

I imagine he hunted with a group on occasion. The shared bounty of cooperative success benefitted all, but he most enjoyed the meat he earned himself.

I like to think the bone, horn, or antler he used to knap the flint and obsidian that tipped his spears came from an animal he took on a solo hunt. Not just a tool, but a story and a memory as well, its history making it feel good in his hand.

When younger, stronger men began to seek his advice rather than his help, he understood and remembered when he was in their place. He showed them how to shape the angles on their stone blades needed to keep edges sharp but still strong. He described how to pick up a track when the blood trail dwindled. And he would hunt on his own. He wouldn't range as far as before, but far enough to get just a little lost on occasion.

We are fortunate enough to have most of the benefits that being alive in modern America allows. I can eat anytime and nearly anything I want. If I'm too cold or too warm, I can, at the touch of a button, alter my environment. I travel long distances in comfort, and if I'm sick or injured I have resources to alleviate my suffering, or almost any inconvenience.

His survival was a daily question. His comfort was at the whim of the elements and his wits. Yet the connection I feel with this man, this hunter, is not diminished by these differences or the millennia.

He and I literally walked the same path. The smell of pine, sage, and entrails were our friends. We savored similar silence, spent September nights treasuring the beauty of familiar constellations and stars, and share a kinship that crosses gender, culture, even time.

I'm grateful to be part of it.

A Fitting Introduction?

"**N**ow that I have some time on my hands, I want to become a fly fisher."

The look on my friend's face was eager, lacking pretense or guile. Despite being a just a year or two younger than my creaky self, he was completely comfortable with the androgynous but so correct "fisher" into which he hoped to evolve.

I kind of envy him. He has so many firsts ahead.

I don't remember catching my first fish, but I have a mental image from that day so clear, I can see it like a photo. I was standing outside the hospital where my mom was recovering from surgery. Dad pointed to a window on an upper floor. I stood, tiny, bundled up in a blue plaid jacket, next to our old blue Studebaker Champion and held up a rock sole about the size of my dad's hand. It was already drying out and curling into the shape of a fishhook. I knew my mom was looking proudly down at her two fishermen.

Eventually I realized that Dad had tricked me. Though Mom was in that hospital, she was in no shape to look out a window all day in case I happened by to wave a stiff fish at her from the parking lot. But it was too late. I had found something in fishing that made me happy. Sixty some years later, it persists.

Bob, the aspiring fly fisher, had no such early introduction. Rather than fishing and hunting, Bob had been responsible and productive his whole adult life. Now, at retirement, he felt free to consider frivolity. At a house party where neither antlers on the wall nor outdoor literature in the bookshelves were in evidence, he approached with a cocktail plate of amuse-bouche in one hand with an appropriate red wine in the other, to ask me about fly fishing.

I had so much to tell him. Not just about fly fishing but about tossing a spinner, or calling a bull elk, stalking within bow range of mule deer…and, and pointing dogs, roosterfish, gobbling toms, double guns, recurves, a list of books he must read and trips he must plan, right now. There was no time to lose.

But wait, this wasn't my first hike on the fire up a rookie trail. I was aware of the risks. I've been unjustly accused by several stern women of being a bad influence on their husbands. That's not really fair. I've made valiant and occasionally successful attempts to be a bad influence on the girls and women in my life as well.

Once, at a company Christmas party, I actually overheard a new hunting partner introduce his wife to the spouse of another coworker with the phrase, "You two have a lot in common. You're both mad at Kevin."

That seemed a little harsh, since one now has a mounted Canada goose in her entryway and the other, not only got her first freezer full of venison that year, but also a neat little black-tail antler coat rack in her foyer.

You're welcome!

Anyway, once burned and all that, plus I've learned a few things over the years.

For example, the guy whose wife now enjoys the mounted goose taught me the value of presentation. When he surprised her with this taxidermy treasure, he took the precaution of placing a diamond tennis bracelet around the goose's neck. I thought it disrespectful to the goose, but she seemed to like that mount more than I expected, so all's well, I guess.

I also discovered that not everyone takes to the outdoors at the same rate.

I needed to think a bit about how to proceed with Bob. He is a guy with potential. He's got no obvious ailments. He owns a nice truck, has time on his hands, and is unlikely to get a mysterious call he "just has to take" when the bar bill comes.

Plus, while without more evidence I can't say for sure, I think he's game.

Being game is important. In addition to the odd miffed spouse, I may have broke (old hound guys would never say "broken") a couple of guys off hunting and fishing because I misjudged their overall level of enthusiasm.

Dean was a one timer. In my defense, I was quite young when I took him on his first, ultimately his last, hunt. We were in college, thin, strong, in shape, things I still remember fondly. Though I may have pushed him a little hard for a rookie, his lack of gumption was disappointing. We walked a long time but at a relaxed, hunting pace. By mid-afternoon he was already complaining. He "was hot" and "so thirsty." Yeah, it was warm for October, and the uneven ground was a little tricky, but it was mostly downhill. Water is heavy so, under the circumstances, seemed an unnecessary burden; besides, I was pretty sure the canyon we were descending in those happy pre-GPS days would end at the Snake River…which is, obviously, water. We had dropped his car at 4:00 that morning before driving my truck to the top of what I assumed was the same canyon. I wouldn't have done that if I wasn't confident. It turned out I was right. The canyon was longer than I'd assumed, but probably not over ten miles—at least not much over. It wasn't even very dark, maybe still legal shooting hours, when we found his car, and the river, yet he was still grumpy. I'd reached the car some time before Dean. When he finally arrived, the things he suggested I do with my rifle and hunting in general seemed inappropriate and rude. In retrospect, I don't think I deserve all the blame for that being his only deer hunt. Dean apparently wasn't cut out to be a hunter.

Jim was a tough guy. I didn't expect he'd come up short. We were deer hunting when I spotted a raccoon sleeping in a Doug Fir. Jim was new to hunting and fishing, so I suspected he'd never before had the opportunity to snatch a coon out of a tree. Being inclined toward sharing, I let him have this turn. I pointed up the tree, then gave him some experience-based tips: "When you grab a coon, you gotta keep 'em moving…sort of swing 'em around or else they'll loop back on you and grab your arm. You don't want that."

Even armed with good instruction, he looked tentative. He climbed okay at first, though slower than I'd hoped. He was still a couple of arm lengths from contact when the coon opened his eyes, looked at Jim, then headed up. Jim followed, at an even more sluggish pace, then petered out completely when the trunk got thin enough to start swaying. For a while Jim and the coon rocked gently back and forth in the tree top then, despite my encouragement, and still several feet below the coon, he gave up the chase.

The next August, Jim and I were wading a summer steelhead river in cutoffs and tennis shoes. An elk trail skirted a shallow riffle that was unlikely to contain fish, so we were a couple of yards from the river, slogging through salmon berry bushes and alders, when we encountered the wasp nest. I admit I didn't, and don't, like getting stung, and yes, synchronized swan dives into 18 inches of water then tumbling downstream was…bumpy. But it was a warm day, so the quick immersion was nice, neither of us had more than a few stings and, though bruised a bit, no rods, reels, or bones were broken. And, we, well I, caught a steelhead that day. So, on balance a win.

Jim golfs now.

Another friend's response was just the opposite.

Steve Duncan and I calculated we hadn't seen each other for nineteen years when we, via a cross-country phone call, decided to get together in Mexico for a few days of marlin fishing, something I had never done. One evening, to anesthetize our fish weary muscles, we were standing hip deep in the Sea of Cortez. With one hand gently sloshing the warm water to stir up bioluminescence, the other holding an icy concoction containing bananas and rum, I broke the starlit silence and said, "You know, Steve, we oughta go to Alaska and do a float trip for caribou." He drained the last mouthful from his glass, was quiet a beat or two longer than seemed necessary, then nodded and said, "Yeah, let's do that."

Our caribou hunt the following August involved a 110-mile drift down a river that didn't have quite enough water to always keep us afloat. The lack of depth required us to regularly get out to slide our loaded raft over the rocks. We spent most of one day dragging the raft back upstream after mistakenly drifting down a dead-end braid. The water was too deep to wade and too much current to row, so to return to the main channel, we lined our raft upstream by shouldering our way through head high brush on a narrow trail along the bank. The trail was slippery and smelly with half-eaten salmon, and other salmon bits which had already been processed by grizzlies. We felt compelled to sing showtunes, as loud as we could.

To supplement our dried rations, we ate ptarmigan, fish, and one evening late in the trip, Steve grilled tenderloin medallions from a beautiful bull caribou, his first big game animal.

On that hunt, I inhaled more and larger mosquitoes than I ever knew existed, survived the two most terrifying plane rides of my life, got soaked, bug bit, and scared. We even got to experience an exciting close-range bluff charge by a sow griz with cubs.

It was great!

Based upon my experience with less avid beginners, I feared Steve might have had enough. I underestimated him by a mile. He has since travelled the world, hunting places and game I've only read about, and just the other day we started talking about cashing in our accumulated Colorado deer preference points.

I needn't have worried. He's game.

Steve's response to my proposal of a trip is the big component of being game. It's not how good one may be at something, it's how willing.

Danny, like Steve, once responded to a pronghorn hunt I suggested without a hundred questions or a dozen caveats, just a quick, "Okay."

Danny's outdoor tastes and mine aren't exactly the same, but they have considerable overlap. Since that first pronghorn trip, and largely because of it, we've shared adventures and campfires for four decades.

Our trips don't always result in the most fish, birds, or the biggest antlers, but Danny is always good to go. Despite his modest tonnage of game over the years, that attitude, that gusto, has translated into great smoked fish; a terrific whitetail on his wall; and a lifetime of fun, stories, and shared, cherished memories.

I haven't fished with Bob yet. I loaned him several books, recommended a guide who can save him years of trial and error in learning about both fly casting and reading a river, and I told him of a few uncrowded but not exactly secret spots to try out his new skills and gear.

And I sent him a note that said,

"I'm happy for you, getting into fishing. Both fishing and hunting offer the tangible rewards everyone understands, fighting

a fish, eating a fish, and eating wild meat, but it's the intangibles that last and prompt the next adventure. I often reflect upon my most memorable moments afield; rarely do they have anything to do with what I caught or shot. But, without the pull of the hunt or the chance to fight a fish, I wouldn't have been there when the grizzly charged. I never would have watched a doe give birth, nor had a several minute stare down with a cougar three steps away. I would have missed seeing a mink steal my trout, or the fox that snatched, then ran off with my only duck of the day. All these perfect moments shared with the best people I know.

You're in for a great adventure."

And he is…if he's game.

Echoes of Old Tom

I was in line at the campus bookstore with a new semester's worth of textbooks under my arm when a book on display caught my eye: *A Hunter's Fireside Book*. I knew the author from his columns in *Sports Afield*, so I knew I'd pass the time more pleasantly in the company of Gene Hill.

There are 76 stories in that book. They range from a single paragraph to several pages. There are 162 pages in all. With odds of 162 to 1, I opened the book to page 57. I found there, a complete story in six paragraphs. It was titled "Old Tom."

Old Tom was about an elderly hunter who, when faced with the realization that his dog Tom needed to be put down, took him hunting one last time, without regard for the season.

"March or no, the old man took vigil near the swamp that night and marked down two or three birds as they came in to roost. And promptly at six the next morning the two gentlemen marched down together through the morning mist, as they had done countless times before…and as one of them hoped they would do countless times again in some other fields."

Well!

Nikki, the dog who had been my constant companion since my seventh birthday, had died just a couple weeks before. I was still missing her terribly, and here I was trapped in a checkout line surrounded by other eighteen to twenty-two-year-olds, many of whom were GIRLS. As my eyes started to spill over, with sudden inspiration, I clutched my belly, feigning imminent vomit, a hangover being legitimate cover. I flung the books under a fabric-draped table to retrieve later, then, forfeiting my spot near the front of the long line, bolted out of the Bookie.

Even outside the potential for embarrassment was everywhere, but once the evidence of my emotion dried, I began to feel better.

Losing my dog hurt…a lot. But maybe my grief wasn't weird. It was comforting to know Gene Hill understood me. If he did, probably so did lots of others. I'd had great years with Nik. This epiphany was beginning to, at least intellectually, help me understand that never having another dog, just to avoid feeling this way, maybe wasn't a solid plan.

After Nikki, I had a Plott, a Black and Tan, two generations of Treeing Walkers, and a Lab—good dogs all, but in a backyard kennel not against my knee. I was forty and the father of a teenage girl and nine-year-old twin boys before I got another dog that lived in my house.

My wife Laurie (my girlfriend in college—she went back to the Bookie and bought me a copy of *A Hunters Fireside Book* that day on campus when my macho façade shattered) was of two minds about an inside dog. She wavered from not liking the idea to hating it. When we picked out Archie, he had the shortest hair of all the pups, thus was her favorite.

Arch was a lucky draw. From the Wirehaired Pointing Griffon Club of America (now called Cesky Fousek North America), he was the product of decades of sound, on purpose breeding decisions, and I strove to do my part. I collected training advice like boot socks collect cheat grass. In a remarkably short time, I had a better hunting dog than I had any right to expect. I learned from Arch, or rather relearned, that the value of a bird dog is less due to his hunting prowess than in the delight a dog adds to the household on the hundreds of days a year I don't hunt. But the hunting was good, too, real good. Arch paved the way for his successors by enhancing my time afield and showing Laurie that shed hair and occasionally muddy feet are a great trade in return for life with a dog.

By the time Archie was eight, the kids he'd helped Laurie and me raise were growing up. Our little girl was a junior in college, and the departure of the guys for a distant campus was on the horizon. It was time for an additional dog, a pup to learn from Archie.

Bogan, another Fousek, came to us that May. Archie nipped his face the first day to establish the rules and hierarchy, then accepted the role of mentor. By the time Bogan passed his puppyhood, he was a proficient bird finder. Bog (long "o" like soda) lacked the grace that drew the eye when Archie devoured the canyon country where we chased quail and chukars, but he hunted hard, was solid on point, retrieved well, and had the helpful quirk of pointing coveys with his head high as though posing at Westminster, and singles with his shoulder blades forming a V above his withers and his chin nearly touching the ground.

I have a mental snapshot of the two of them pointing the same small covey of Valley Quail. There was just enough snow to cover the ground and sprinkle the sage brush. Bogan stood frozen, head high. Arch twisted in a crouch looking back over his left shoulder. The two of them, wirehaired statues against a backdrop of frosted Russian Olives and sage. That happened just once.

Bogan got hit by a car. He was knocked down but got right up. I wasn't home when it happened, and he looked okay, but I still walked him to our neighbor Keith, who was also our vet.

Other than a mild concussion and sore ribs, it appeared Bogan was uninjured.

It was a year before the first seizure.

It was ugly and violent. Bog's legs churning then tightening, twisting into rigor mortis-like stiffness, lips drawn in a grimace, chuffing and spraying foam from his mouth, and surprisingly noisy.

When I took him to the doc that time, Keith suggested we watch him. "Dogs are allowed one seizure before we start looking for a cause," he said.

After a few months, the appalling rigidity and all over wetness of the event was barely a memory.

The next seizure was worse. I don't know if it was physically more brutal, but now it was part of who Bogan was.

As the years passed, I gave Bogan pills, liquid meds, too. With a pharmacist's help, we'd tweak the dosage, trying to reach the perfect level that would eliminate seizures without drugging him up too much. Laurie and I kept a Tupperware container full of hot dog slices in the fridge. I'd stuff a pill or a couple pills into a slice and hand him his "treat." It wasn't long before pill camo became unnecessary. He'd take each tiny white pill and eagerly swallow it as though he knew it was the source of his buzz.

The combination of seizures and drugs diminished him physically but revealed his true nature. Bogan was the world's nicest dog. The drugs and wear from his epilepsy seemed only to amplify his innate niceness.

Though the drugs diminished the seizures, they destroyed his inhibition. He would take food, napkins, even a fork from any hand or plate he could reach. Once he looked me right in the eye with pure love while lifting his leg and peeing on my coffee table.

During seizures, which ranged from occasional to a record six in one day, he leaked. There was always urine and saliva but, due to his convulsions, I never knew for sure which was the source of wetness on his back. When the ominous thumping of a new seizure would start, then build like a giant grouse drumming, I'd run to carry him outside to minimize the moist, while Laurie grabbed towels to cushion his head.

I'd sit with him until the worst was over. When the gyrations ceased, he'd doze for a while, usually followed by a sort of manic phase where he'd do laps around the yard. When he finished this run, he'd sleep again, hard and long.

We replaced our carpet with easier to clean wood. An expense and a hassle, but the pure joy Bogan exuded with people and his old buddy Arch was a lesson in the lemons into lemonade philosophy. He'd wake from a nap, walk over and gaze into my eyes with such a sense of anticipation that sometimes I just laughed. Other than his bath-proof stench, he was a pleasure to be around.

We joked that he started every sentence with "Dude," but he loved life. He was consistently happy and constantly high. In the evenings he'd climb up on my lap, sigh deeply, then dig his nose under my chin or armpit, then sleep, reeking and snoring in his special way, as long as I'd let him stay.

I still took him hunting. He'd forgotten what he knew about the uplands, but he'd fetch a duck if it splashed dead and close, and he loved to go.

A 65-pound dog seizing in a dog box in a Suburban sounds like a flat tire and makes the cab smell like our house before the wood floors, but I had to take him. Archie was retired by the time Bogan achieved full drug-addled loony status, so I decided to take Bog on one last big "him and me" trip. We went to a place in Montana where I was pretty sure I could shoot a few pheasants without his help. Both my partners on this trip had young dogs who needed the work, so a long drive to productive pheasant country was good for us all.

It was pretty much as I expected. I covered a lot of ground with Bogan happily at my side. When a songbird passed close by, he'd lope after it for a few seconds then return to me grinning. He was always so surprised and pleased at the noise and commotion when I'd flush a pheasant. He still loved the sound of shotgun fire; when I shot, he'd do his rocking horse run along the general course of the bird and flail around excitedly. When he did stumble across a bird I'd shot, he'd pin it to the ground with his front paws and enthusiastically start yanking out feathers. Plucking was a new idea, and he seemed genuinely proud of it.

On the last morning of our hunt, Bog and I were strolling through a grassy patch surrounded by some heavily grazed ground when a rooster jumped up. I almost whiffed, just winged him. The bird hit the ground running in cover barely taller than his spurs. The chase was on! I was so happy for Bog; he had a long sight chase that ended with a form tackle in an explosion of dust. Bogan was thrilled to be enveloped in a cloud of feathers and was trying desperately to finish plucking his prize before I caught up.

I tucked the nearly naked rooster into my vest, then evaluated my old buddy. He'd just had a serendipitous end to what I'd come to accept was his last hunt. I thought he'd be tuckered out by his big day, but he still seemed to have a little go, so we walked the brushy margin of a dry creek, our path straight into a slight breeze.

Bogan started working out front: head high, quartering, nose into the wind. After several seasons, as well as the past five days of walking beside or behind me, he was now 40 yards ahead working the breeze, sorting for the tantalizing whiff of pheasant among the deer and tweety birds. The years of drugs and sickness sloughing away, I saw him get birdy, creeping, his tail up and stiff but still moving. Then he stopped. More rigid than his worst seizure, magnificent against the sun-colored grass, shoulder blades in relief, chin barely an inch off the ground, tail barely quivering. One last time, everything he'd almost been and all he was meant to be. I strode into position facing him, the bird between us. With no other movement, he raised his eyes, locking them onto mine. "There's a bird here, boss. I got him."

I thought of Old Tom. I was certain what was about to happen, and I knew what I would do for my dog, my friend, for both of us. His gaze returned to the grass. I stepped in to flush.

When the hen clattered out, I shot her. Bogan was on her in an instant. He plucked her clean.

Collateral Grouse

"I didn't get an elk, but I got a couple grouse," I said in response to the question bowhunters have all heard in small towns throughout the west when we stop for gas and Cheetos while wearing camo.

"You carry a sidearm, do ya?" the proprietor of the gas n go continued.

"No, I got 'em with my bow."

His look of surprise is something I'm used to. Most western bowhunters have probably shot more grouse than elk while chasing antlers, but non-hunters and gun-only guys seem to equate killing a bird with an arrow as magic, pure luck, or an outright lie.

I would agree if I were shooting them on the wing, but grouse can be pretty accommodating. They often sit as I mosey into comfortable range. I did almost get a ruffed grouse on the wing once. During a late deer season, I was creeping up a draw when I spotted a ruff in a tangle of alders 10–12 steps up the cut. I always keep my grouse arrow in the same spot in my quiver so I could ease it out and on to my string without taking my eyes off the grouse. As I drew, he flushed but flew straight up the draw. I barely adjusted my bow arm to account for the flush, released, watched as the arrow slid by, it seemed, just under an outstretched wing…then smashed into the rocky hillside.

Arrows are often casualties when bowhunting grouse, but there are ways to decrease the cost and frustration of broken and lost arrows.

The first thing all aspiring grouse hunters should know is that field points and broadheads are not grouse arrows. If you are going to kill a grouse, you want to eat it. For any ethical hunter, recovery of the game, whatever it is, is paramount. Pointy arrowheads zip through a grouse seemingly surrendering only a fraction of their velocity.

Before I learned this lesson, I put a field point through a blue grouse on a ridgeline below me. It was within my range and, I swear, he looked as big as a young turkey. My shot was perfect, I thought. I hit the big blue in the middle of his back. The arrow passed through then sailed out over the canyon followed a second later by the mortally wounded grouse, which flapped a couple beats, then set its wings and sailed out of sight into the timber a thousand feet below.

Even with an appropriate judo or a blunt, grouse recovery can be challenging.

A big blue grouse standing on the grassy side of an abandoned road is something that doesn't take a lot of thought, and with the right shot recovery is usually easy. If you are mentally tough enough to limit yourself to this kind of shot, well, good for you, but I'm not. I have shot more grouse, of all kinds, with my bow, out of trees than I ever have on the ground.

A grouse in a tree is a tempting target. Sometimes that seductive silhouette is just too much to even stop and consider. You feel you must act, and right now! You will miss this shot. You will also lose your arrow.

During practice you don't often get to see an arrow arcing out of sight like that. It is impressive, especially against a sunny blue sky, but it's a rookie mistake. One I've replayed many times, for decades.

A grouse in the tree is an equation you must solve. While concentrating on the required calculations, you will often be interrupted by a flush. This is okay because after the first miss, the one that sent your arrow into the ozone, if you don't slow down and do the geometry, it's easy to send more arrows after the first.

When shooting at a perched bird, you want something to stop your arrow in the event of a miss; however, an arrow stuck into a tree where you can't reach it is just as gone as those you launch into the sky. There is also the chance you'll hit the bird. Usually, the combination of the impact of the arrow and subsequent flapping of wings will topple your bird out of a tree, but sometimes you have to climb.

Most of the time when presented with this situation, I try to line up the bird with the trunk of the tree it's in, or one right next to it. Occasionally a backstop of a bunch of branches will look thick and intertwined enough that I'm confident a prong or two of my judo point will catch. Sometimes it does.

So, when you find a grouse, get within comfortable range, have the right point (judo or blunt), angle for a good backstop, and make the shot you're on the way to one of the best camp meals you'll have. There can be another step in this process though. Sometimes you have to track your bird.

Last fall, I had two consecutive days with tricky grouse recoveries. I lined up my shot on a big blue in a tree, had the appropriate backstop, and made a good shot. I heard a distinct pop on impact and could see that the arrow didn't penetrate like it usually does. I'd center punched the gizzard. Despite being hit hard, the grouse was able to fly rather than fall from the tree. It flew out at an angle that put some distance between us. I saw it hit and run, but it disappeared into the huckleberries, lupine, and trees. Standing still and listening will often reveal a wounded grouse flapping its final wingbeats. This time I got nothing.

I eventually found him, but it took a while. The gizzard hit left him mobile. When I recovered him, he was nearly 30 yards from where I'd lost sight of him and had made a 90 degree turn from the path he'd been on. I'm not certain I would have found him if not for my bright yellow and white fletching.

The next day I shot a spruce grouse. Spruce grouse are a problem. Blues and ruffs usually fly when you miss them; spruce grouse look around, shuffle their feet, then dare you to shoot again. I suspect I've lost more arrows on spruce grouse than ruffs, blues, and ptarmigan combined. To make it worse, I much prefer eating ruffs and blues. I usually save my spruce grouse for stir fry or tacos. I suspect there is a correlation with the wariness of a bird and their tastiness (see mergansers).

My first miss resulted in a lost arrow. I recovered a second arrow but left the judo point in my backstop tree. I killed the bird with the third shot. Shots number two and three required me to remove a broadhead from an elk arrow and replace it with a judo point. As I did all this, the cock bird bobbed his head and watched me.

This bird also got a flying start rather than just falling, but after hitting the ground, he ran a few steps then flew away. I stood staring—couldn't believe it. I spent a long time looking for my arrow. When I finally found it, the fletching was still in an unmistakably dead grouse. The flush had been a second bird I hadn't seen.

My most memorable recovery was a big cock blue grouse in a fir tree. It was a big tree. The grouse was at least forty feet off the ground; however, the hill was steep. My perch on the berm of the logging road left me just slightly below bird level. Those big blues are tough. I saw the impact, then he took off, taking my arrow along with him. My buddy Mike and I searched for long time, made wider and wider circles, but eventually gave up.

We got back to the truck and headed for home. We had a lot of elevation to lose, so the road switchbacked down the mountain. An hour and a half after my shot, probably a quarter mile as the grouse flies, and two switchbacks down the mountain, we found my grouse, my arrow still in him, dead in the middle of the road.

Grouse, all of them, are beautiful birds. Their fans on a wall or in a photo make nice keepsakes, but above all, we shoot grouse because they are so darn good to eat.

The first time I ever shot grouse for camp meat rather than taking them home worked out really well. My partner on that trip was a much more savvy and experienced hunter than me. We were elk hunting in an Idaho wilderness area and had packed for sustenance rather than fine dining. The addition of grouse breast converted our Top Ramen from boring but light weight and easy to carry noodles into a memorable feast.

Since that time, on multi-day trips, I try to remember to pack a tiny bottle of olive oil. If I don't feel like grouse for a main course, sautéed cubes of grouse breast with a light sprinkle of salt are a fine way to start an evening in camp.

When hunting elk and deer, as I wander, I envision screaming bulls and thick necked bucks. They are, after all, why I'm in the mountains or the forests. But if there were no grouse in all their different species and color phases, my deer hunting would be diminished, my elk camps less memorable, and my palate less satisfied.

Though grouse are often an afterthought, they are a very good thought indeed.

Happy Wanderer

"Okay Kev, you sit here watching this meadow while Bruce and I make a big loop on the horses. We'll be back in a couple of hours."

"If I just sit here for two hours, I'll explode!"

My guide's plan was a good one, and if I'd listened to him, I might have killed a moose on that trip. In my defense, I was a twenty-three-year-old hothead, and since I had forked over a full $600 for a week of moose hunting, I wanted to be "hunting." To me that meant covering ground, not staring at an empty meadow.

I was a knucklehead on that 1970s hunt. I had strong opinions based on stunningly scant experience. I was carrying a rifle on that trip. In addition to being adamant about not sitting still, I was pretty sure hunters who used scopes or slings were weenies. Within just a year or two, I reevaluated my scope and sling position, but my preference for wandering rather than sitting still remains intact.

I understand the benefits of a blind or stand. I have friends who swear by their tree stands and whose antler walls have more points than a porcupine. The size of some of those antlers is noteworthy as well.

Another friend of mine has left boot tracks all over North America by being as tough or tougher than the elk, deer, grizzlies, or whatever game he's pursuing at the time. After decades of spot and stalk hunting with his bow, he's converted to tree stands almost exclusively. "I get better shots," he explained.

The first time I tried a tree stand should have converted me. It was a self-climber, a simple contraption with brown Astroturf stapled to a plywood platform. I was hunting an area new to me, so I slung it over my shoulder and started walking. Fatigue more than careful study led me to choose where to hang my first ever tree stand. I shinnied up a pine, dragging the contraption up the tree with my toes. About ten feet up, I figured that was enough and slammed my heels down hard enough to give me confidence the stand would stay put, then settled in.

On that cold December morning, I didn't even have time to cool off and shiver. The southeastern Washington buck that strolled by just minutes later was not the biggest whitetail I'd ever seen, but years later, remains near the top of that list. He was too far away for a shot but was headed my way. His path arced, then brought him within the outside edge of my range. He stopped with his head and those handsome antlers hidden behind a pine. Another tree trunk hid his back half, neatly framing the spot I expected to put an arrow.

Other than Murphy's Law, or maybe a touch of buck fever, I can't explain how I hit wood rather than lungs. When that Bear Razorhead smacked into the tree, it sounded like a solid double off a major league bat. The buck bolted but stopped before I lost sight of him. He stood for a while, his tail still bristling but parallel to his back rather than waving flamboyantly as it had just moments before. He looked around and then dropped his head to reacquire the track of what I assume was the estrous doe that had brought him to me in the first place.

In addition to my new tree stand, I was equipped with my first ever grunt call. I squeezed my bow between my knees, brought the call to my lips, and blew gently. I should have practiced with the grunt tube—all I got was a hiss. The buck didn't react at all. I was able to regroup and remember to inhale on the mouthpiece, which I did, producing a credible grunt. That stopped him. I don't remember how long our dance lasted, but for several minutes every time he'd turn his back and start to leave, my grunt would turn him. He never quite made it close enough for a redemption shot, but it was a surprising and enlightening experience.

That should have been a turning point for me. Despite whacking a tree, I'd had a close encounter with a mature buck that never knew I was there. The stand gave me an edge in my visibility and put me above where the deer would expect danger. The grunt tube prolonged my encounter with this buck, and nearly gave me one of those infrequent second chances we all crave after a miss. This was not only a way to more venison, hunting from the stand was fun because I had that buck so close and unaware.

When I met my partner back at our wall tent later that day, I shared my exciting story. I was fired up, it was so easy. I fell asleep that night looking forward to spending the next day in a tree. When I awoke the following morning, I looked at my stand leaning against the tire of my truck, considered hills and meadows I had not yet seen, then left it where it was. Despite the previous day's lesson, I still preferred creeping through the countryside looking for game rather than waiting for it to come to me.

Slipping over a hogback and seeing antler tips masquerading as branches protruding from sagebrush appeals to me. The satisfaction I get from stalking within range of a buck I spotted a half mile away is, I suspect, similar to the feeling of perfectly placing a stand to take advantage of wind and studied travel routes. I don't pretend my sometimes aimless meandering is a superior method of hunting. On the contrary, I've told friends if I needed meat I'd be in a stand. I am, however, reconsidering my strategy. I've tossed plenty of unnotched tags, and high miles knees have diminished my range. Consequently, when, one recent December, my friend Todd offered me use of his permanent ground blind and guidance to an appropriate tree, I decided it was time to give stands another try.

In a nod to the times, I bought a packable ladder to get me up a tree and a current model tree stand sporting a metal rather than a plywood platform. I also acquired a safety harness, which, much like scopes and slings, I had considered superfluous and a bit wimpy before my brain developed.

Todd lives in great game country in northeastern Washington. He shares the neighborhood with moose, mule deer, whitetails, and elk as well as sufficient predators to keep those antlered animals in check. When I arrived midday after a long drive, he was waiting for me. We drove, then hiked the last bit to his whitetail spot. I hadn't given much thought to what I expected, but I was surprised to see a plywood shack with a shooting hole and a lawn chair inside. From there he led me the quarter mile to the tree he'd chosen for me. With hanging the stand, then cutting shooting lanes through the branches, it took longer than I'd expected to get my tree stand squared away. Once it was set and I was perched in the tree, Todd left me with good wishes and a promise that his wife Judy would feed me later.

He disappeared among the pines, and before long normal bird and squirrel sounds resumed. I settled in and waited, ready for a buck to appear. After twenty minutes with no action, I was restless. The last time I sat in a stand it didn't take this long, not even close. I looked around and realized that almost every tree

I could see looked like a better spot than where I was, and just over the hill there were probably bucks just wandering around. Finally, since nothing was going on, I was clearly in the wrong tree, and I was bored, it occurred to me that I should practice drawing my bow.

I'd cleared branches during the set up so I didn't think there would be an issue, but better to check now than to foul things up in the unlikely event a buck showed up. I stood, plucked my bow from the branch on which it was hanging and, as I drew, the platform beneath my feet seemed to shrink while the distance to the ground increased. I eased off on the bowstring then sat right back down to consider this. Apparently shooting from a tree stand is an acquired skill, or perhaps more accurately for me, a fear to overcome.

Uninterrupted by deer, I practiced standing and drawing in several directions. By dark I believed I could shoot from the stand, although with a persistent pucker factor slightly altering my form.

The next morning, I chose the ground blind. Todd and his son Matt had each killed bucks and passed on several others from this same spot, so I waited with confidence. I did see a couple of does that morning. Although they were legal, I was in buck mode, and they never came close enough to test my resolve.

For the next several days, I alternated between the tree and the ground blind, preferring the visibility from the tree but appreciating the warmth and shelter from the intermittent wind, snow, and sleet provided by the shack. By the time of this December hunt, the rut activity had waned. Periodic howling was never really close, but wolf tracks dimpled the snow within yards of the shack. Though according to reports, the wolves prefer moose to deer. I suspect their proximity may have had something to do with the lack of deer relative to Matt and Todd's experience a few weeks earlier. They both had passed up bucks before letting an arrow loose. I was still hoping to see a buck, but if a doe gave me a chance, I was ready to take it.

That chance finally came on my last afternoon. After a cold morning in the tree, at mid-day I opted for the shelter of the shack. I was in the lawn chair peeking out when two does appeared. As they approached, I quietly slid from the lawn chair to a kneeling position. I watched and waited with several inches of my arrow protruding from the shooting window. When the larger of the two exposed her chest I drew, touched the corner of my mouth, and let fly.

The window had seemed a bit small and the angle awkward, but that's why I knelt. The compounds Matt and Todd shot worked well there, but when I dropped the string of my 62-inch recurve, both limbs slammed into the plywood walls. The crash of bow to wood and the jarring impact in my hand and up my arm may have led me to add to the racket with a loud, rude, though appropriate comment. The commotion was enough to send the deer on their way, leaving my arrow lying impotently near the blind.

That was how my reintroduction to stand hunting ended.

That was two years ago. I was talking to Todd the other day, and he invited me back. If I don't sneak up on a deer and fill my tag this fall, I may be back up a tree, or in a shack this winter. This time I'll make a point to be farther from the wall. I'm kind of looking forward to it.

Glitches

"It was a nightmare," I heard Laurie say.

I turned to listen as my wife, between sips of Pinot Grigio, continued her harrowing description of the perils she'd faced on a British Columbia salmon fishing trip from which we'd recently returned.

Others at the barbeque, drawn by her tone, naturally drifted her way. An adventure story of this magnitude was too compelling to ignore.

"It took HOURS to get to the camp, and the road was dusty and terrible…it was so rough, things were breaking off our boat!"

There were gasps, laughter, and universal amazement as her story of woe unfolded.

Some of the amazement was mine.

Okay, I admit getting there took longer than I'd planned, and the road was…bumpy. The extended pounding on that washboard surface may have been the reason the spare tire mount sheared off the boat trailer. And, when the screws rattled out and one of the guide bunks fell off, it was no real problem. I slowed down so the boat never really shifted to what a fair observer would call a dangerous extent. As for the spare snapping off, we clearly saw the tire as it passed us, so it was an easy retrieve from where its momentum ran out on the side of the road. Had it bounced just a little farther, the fast-rolling tire would have sailed into an impressively steep and deep canyon. It didn't. I call that a win.

Apparently, I'd been so gentle with Laurie for so long her perspective had been warped. Other than the salmon mysteriously disappearing from what is a normally productive spot, this trip was easy and mostly trouble free. We stayed in an actual campground. From our site it was a relatively short walk to indoor plumbing, and right there, in the campground, was a little store featuring bait, beer, and ice cream bars. The garbage cans were bear proof. With all the fancy amenities, once the tent was up, it was hard to distinguish our camp from a hotel. The head nets I'd brought weren't even necessary, with the mosquitos being almost as scarce as the salmon.

I had to face the fact that I'd treated my bride of several decades to too much luxury and pampering. It had been some time since Laur had helped pack a deer out of a canyon or jumped off a cliff into a river.

In the days following our return from Vancouver Island, a number of holes opened in conversation. I'm pretty sure I was expected to grab a shovel full of apology to fill them in.

Several times, in the spirit of marital bliss, I considered making an attempt, but I just couldn't do it.

I've had trips where everything happened exactly as planned—at least I assume I have. I don't recall much about them. I probably caught fish, shot some pheasants, or had a dry sunny float, but an excursion lacking adjustments on the fly, random opportunities to improvise, or moments of pure adrenaline-driven panic just doesn't have much staying power in my memory.

I like spice in my food, rapids in my rivers, and conflict in the novels I read. I certainly don't want my outdoor adventures to be bland, beige, boring, or devoid of uncertainty.

If the drive to that Vancouver Island fishing camp had been a half a day shorter on a smooth road, it would have been easier but, considering the lack of fish, a pleasant but utterly forgettable trip.

Thanks to a couple of minor issues, I don't think that trip will be forgotten any time soon.

Issues, hassles, hiccups, and glitches are all part of a continuum that add zest to our jaunts off the pavement, and spark to our stories. Hiccups to a degree and glitches for sure, will alter attitudes and make memories.

Glitches differ from hiccups. A hiccup barely rises above a hassle and is based on something mundane. Multiple flat tires, overly inquisitive customs agents, poor planning, etc. A hiccup is annoying and wastes time but is soon forgotten.

A glitch is different. It appears out of nowhere. It's completely unanticipated, and generates concern, even momentary conviction, that disaster is imminent. A good glitch often begins with some variant of "Holy Excrement!" being shouted in a lively manner, often accompanied by involuntary arm waving. Ultimately heroic action or luck saves the day.

Glitches don't cause irreparable harm but are a visceral reminder that catastrophe is possible.

I've never had things go terribly wrong. Occasional close calls are inevitable, but in all my years afield there has only been one immediate visit to a medical facility…well, two, no, maybe five or six counting dogs, but rattlesnakes and porcupines are just part of the landscape, not glitches per se.

Most trip-initiated doctor visits could be put off, at least for the duration of the adventure.

Speaking of doctors, taking one along seems like a good idea. Like having a flashlight or a knife. As I learned in Boy

Scouts, it's good to be prepared. It turns out they're not always as handy as you'd expect.

Six of us planned to canoe a beautiful stretch of a designated Wild and Scenic River. In three days, we intended to float sixty miles to the take out, where our shuttled trucks would be waiting. An unexpected heavy rain postponed our departure by a day, so we were eager to get on the river.

Fred, the lone physician on the trip, his teenage son Andy, and I had plenty of river miles on other waters, but we had not floated this river. We were experienced, confident, and somewhat competent. John, Greg, and Tony lacked our canoeing background but were enthusiastic. John manned the bow of my canoe, while Tony and Greg partnered up.

In retrospect, some might say that assigning rookies Tony and Greg "the green canoe" could be called self-serving. But there was a reason Fred and I had bought canoes designed for rivers. Besides, the green canoe would probably be just fine.

We all put in at the same time, but before long four of us were drifting comfortably downstream in the brisk current while the guys in the green canoe were falling behind. Soon they were out of sight.

A sandy beach with an easy eddy on river left beckoned. It looked like a nice spot to stretch our legs while waiting for the newbies to catch up. After a vigil long enough to incite brow furrowing, yet a bit short of foreboding, Andy, our sharp-eyed teenage crew member, pointed into the current and said, "That's a bad sign."

The lone Birkenstock drifting in the current was momentary cause for concern, but in the time it took for us to exchange worried looks, Tony and Greg swept into sight, heads bobbing merrily alongside their capsized canoe. Other than soaked gear and just the one missing sandal, everything was fine.

Due to our expertise and general goodwill, Fred and I offered some pointers about how to keep the green side down, but Tony and Greg appeared uninterested in our advice. The exaggerated rattle of their chattering teeth seemed a bit over the top.

We emptied the water from their canoe, and in no time our whole fleet was once again all upright and pointed downstream.

We soon passed beneath a bridge which was the threshold to the official Wild and Scenic section of the river. The next road access was nearly 50 miles away with nothing between but beautiful solitude and scenery.

I blame what happened next on a combination of the rain enhanced river, excessive gravity, hydraulics, and possibly a tiny miscalculation on my part. The constantly soggy Greg and Tony suggested Karma.

As we approached the first significant rapid, the others pulled over to watch as John and I picked the best route to lead the way. We paddled into the top of the chute, dug in our paddles, and barely missed a perfect line. As we raced toward a house-sized rock, each standing wave we climbed was taller than its predecessor. Newton's third law of motion would predict that the drop into the trough on the back of those waves would be deeper, too.

That is a valid hypothesis.

I calculated later that my canoe can hold approximately 317 gallons of cold river water. Considering the amount John and I swallowed, we'll just round off to 320 gallons, which if you do the math, is really heavy.

In the excitement of the waves and the giant rock, I may have lost count, though I'm pretty sure we were at the crest of the fifth wave, still hanging in, when some quirk of the aforementioned hydraulics and gravity launched John. Even with the distractions, I was able to notice and appreciate the altitude he achieved, and that brief moment of stillness when his upward momentum ran out. He was on his way down, still several feet above the water furiously paddling air when I lost sight of him. Admiring John's surprising exit didn't occupy me for long because the sudden change in weight distribution on board was the checkmate in this chess match between me and the river.

When I eventually surfaced in the flat water below the rapid, John was nearing shore downstream. I kicked toward him. The canoe drifted between us so was an easy retrieve.

After watching John and me scout this rapid, the other two teams opted to line their boats through that stretch.

We reconvened for triage.

Fred, the ever-helpful medical professional, gently palpated the rapidly coloring lump which was later confirmed to be my broken ribs. He bit his lower lip, sucked in a breath, then said, "Man, I bet that hurts."

He would have won that bet.

I nodded.

"Would you call it a searing pain?"

"Yup," I said, without unclenching my teeth.

"We're a couple days from the take out," Fred offered. "What are you going to do about that?"

"I was hoping you might have some thoughts," I said.

He pondered for a moment. "Do you want an aspirin?"

"Is that your best offer?" I asked, but I could tell it was and, again, nodded.

At camp that night it rained again, hampering John's efforts to get a fire going, so, in a flash of inspiration, he poured white gas on the kindling then struck a match.

We all agreed that the ensuing conflagration, though brief, beautifully illuminated John's second unique acrobatic move of the day. The erupting flames singed the hair off his right arm, took most of his right eyebrow, and just enough off the side of his head to give him a jaunty look. The wind and rain somewhat mitigated the unpleasant odor of his charred hair.

Over the next two days, Tony had a flare up of his gout, throbbing ribs hampered my normally elegant paddle strokes, the green canoe capsized regularly, almost as though they had a quota, and someone, I forget who, lost a tooth.

Greg and Tony got much better at balancing when swamped. On the last day, they were still upright when they drifted into the flat water below a series of standing waves. Two guys, no boat in sight, nipple deep, rhythmically paddling a submerged and completely invisible canoe, is an enduring memory from that trip.

When we got home, Greg, Tony, and John all bought canoes, river canoes, none green. Sunshine and a dry ride would not have had the same effect.

Every excursion in the wilds offers an opportunity for luck or mismanagement to suddenly make things memorable. Rivers multiply those options.

Several days into a ten- to twelve-day (depending on flying weather for our bush pilot) Alaska float trip, my buddy Duncan and I agreed that things had gone well despite some modest inconvenience. While it was looking increasingly likely I would be skunked with my recurve bow, Duncan brought a rifle and had tagged a very nice bull caribou. We'd augmented our freeze-dried food with medallions of caribou tenderloin, as well as salmon and ptarmigan. For dessert we had cylinders of tiny cinnamon rolls with extra packages of icing. Days of hunting, fishing, and drifting a true wilderness river had been really fun. Two aspects that could have been improved were the river level and the bugs.

Mosquitos are annoying anywhere, but the number and enthusiasm of the swarms in Alaska around Labor Day exceeded my expectations. Mesh masks, gloves, Deet, and duct tape preserved our sanity, but barely. Even while wearing masks in the zipped-up tent, each bite of our gourmet fare was accompanied by a spoonful of mosquitos, making our food feel almost alive, quivering as it slid down our gullets.

Bugs were a hassle, but, due to our preparation, barely north of an issue. The river wasn't a problem. It was pretty, drifted us through amazing country, and held a variety of willing fish. It was just shallow.

With our gear, a pile of caribou meat, and the two of us, that confluence of weight and low flow left us hanging up on rocks with monotonous regularity. To get going again, the rower would remain in the raft while the other guy slid over the side to drag us to floating depth.

I'd been on the oars for a couple hours. Duncan had been in and out of the boat dozens of times. It was tiring. I didn't blame him for dozing off. He was facing me with his back downstream, his head bobbing in time with my pulls on the oars.

The river began to narrow, providing better clearance over the rocks. I was enjoying the first unimpeded drift we'd had in a while, as well as the increasing speed. We swept around the next bend and saw something I'd been hoping to see but with a bigger buffer.

"Duncan, wake up, there's a grizzly in the river."

He awakened quickly, then spun around in time to see two dog-sized cubs splash into the river alongside their mom.

We both chose the same bad word, uttered quietly but with genuine conviction.

Duncan grabbed the slug-loaded shotgun we had been advised to keep handy, pointed it generally toward the bears, then hollered, "HEY, BEAR!" He wanted to give her time to run away with her babies before we bumped into the three of them with the raft.

Her head snapped our way at his first syllable. She was on her way toward us at an alarming rate before he finished the second. The water remained deep enough for us to maintain our speed but not deep enough to slow the bear.

I cranked the oars trying to decrease the rate at which we were converging, but to little effect. Suddenly she stopped, then stood on her hind legs, with water dripping off the tips of her claws. She swung her uptilted head, apparently catching our scent, decided she'd made her point, huffed, then dropped to all fours and loped ashore followed a moment later by her cubs. As the second cub disappeared into the riverside brush, we drifted into the still roiled water they'd just abandoned. That's when we hung up on the rocks.

The bears were out of sight, but we could hear the sow huffing and see the foliage shake just yards away. Duncan looked at me. I could see him considering the implications of this new development. He would need to hand the shotgun to me, drop into the water, stand on the slippery river bottom, then tug the raft off the rocks. Meanwhile, out of sight, but still just a handful of bear strides away, the absolutely wrong mix of grizzly bears were stomping, blowing, and for all we knew, mom was rethinking her earlier decision.

Once we were free, Duncan hopped in. His fatigue seemingly gone, as I could see daylight under him as he cleared the side of the raft on reentry.

After multiple close encounters with caribou, amazing flights in and out of the Alaskan wilds, and superb fishing, those adrenaline-fueled moments when it was unclear if Duncan, the bear, or I would survive the next few seconds was the highlight of the trip.

Moose aren't as dramatic as bears but can go from goofy looking to glitchy in a hurry.

Al was recovering from hip replacement surgery but decided he could handle an easy trip from our homes in Washington to a favorite spot of mine in British Columbia. It was June, so we could count on seeing black bears, maybe even a griz or two. Seeing early June bears was a sure thing, so was the fishing. Ice out had just occurred so the fish might not be overly eager, but we'd likely catch a few kokanee to eat and enough rainbows to hold our attention. Besides, it was a good chance to get out after a long gray winter.

After a couple of days of watching bears and catching pan-sized trout and kokanee, we opted for a chance at bigger fish. Stu, an old buddy who guides in the area, told me a lake I'd previously only seen from the back of a horse now had a road to it. It was not a good road, but it skirted the bigger mud holes that would sink my truck and would eventually get us to the lake. We were unlikely, Stu told us, to catch many fish, but any we caught would probably be the biggest rainbows of our lives. To make it even more enticing, he had a boat stashed at the lake. All we needed to take was oars.

Clearly a flawless plan. A road, a boat, and giant fish. We were in.

The road was bad, the going slow, but we did get to the lake. The road/trail ended at the shore. Whoever had cut in the vehicle access cleared a spot just big enough, with a little back and forth, to turn around a modest SUV.

As I parked, I said, "Look, Al, there's a moose." It was a yearling.

We watched for a bit, then when it wandered off I went in search of the boat Stu had stashed "Just down the shoreline a ways, eh?" while Al got busy assembling the gear we needed to battle huge trout.

I found the boat.

It was fiberglass, eight feet long with a plastic tractor seat bolted to the center seat. Had the oarlocks been closer to the stern than the seat, it would have been a bad situation—this was much worse. The slots for the oarlocks were slightly behind the seat. Notice I said, "slots for the oarlocks." There was only one oarlock.

However, we were here to fish.

When I got back, Al had our rods set up and ready to go. I concocted a pseudo-oarlock from a vice grip and two bungie cords I found under the seat of my truck. We were set.

Al was gently stepping into the boat when we both reacted to a strange sound.

"ERR, ERR."

The moose running toward us, a cow, appeared to have an agenda. She was in the water just a few feet offshore coming fast. Not an ears back, "I'm being chased by wolves" run, but not much slower. Even with her wide set eyes, she made eye contact like she knew me and held a grudge.

"Run Away! Get to the truck." We were both shouting as we abandoned that ugly little boat and ran for cover. She kept coming, grunting like she was swearing.

"ERR, ERR, ERR," she said.

We watched her come for most of a hundred yards. She didn't slow until she was within 20 feet. The grunting continued as she stalked back and forth. We stood by the open doors of the truck poised to jump in if necessary while yelling at her, throwing rocks and sticks, and honking the horn.

This standoff went on for several minutes.

"ERR."

Honk.

"ERR."

"Git, you darn moose."

"ERR, ERR."

Finally, she walked away, periodically glaring at us over her shoulder.

She had been out of sight for several minutes before we felt confident that leaving the sanctuary of the truck wouldn't provoke another hoo haw with this surly old gal.

With the miserable road, oarlock repair, and hiding from a moose, we'd squandered precious fishing time. We wanted to get going.

In addition to being tiny and ugly, the boat leaked. Not an alarming amount but worth monitoring and taking our coffee cups from the truck for bailing. Despite the torture chamber placement of the oars, I was able to slowly row us out into the middle of the lake. Once there, away from the protective trees, we were able to more fully appreciate the wind. No whitecaps but a good puff. We didn't have much freeboard when we started; we had less now. Water was seeping through the leak at an accelerating rate. Al began to bail; I kept an eye on the waves.

My awkward rowing complicated by wind and chop was enough to tangle our lines.

We reeled in and both bent to the task of undoing the mess we'd made, our heads almost touching.

"Err, err."

Al and I looked at each other, then, simultaneously, swiveled toward the faint but familiar sound.

The shore seemed a long way away. Halfway between us and the shore, a cow moose was swimming toward us. She was grunting.

Just a few seconds of passionate rowing was all either of us needed to understand that outdistancing the moose was not one of our options.

We were well offshore, in a small, leaky pram, mere days after ice-out, and about to be boarded by a moose.

I lifted an oar, the one not strapped in by a vice grip and bungies, and prepared for battle.

I don't know why she changed her mind. Maybe she saw the determination in my eyes, maybe someone had smacked her with an oar the last time she attacked a boat. Whatever the reason, Al and I were mightily pleased when she turned toward shore.

We never got a bite that day, but in the short time we were on that lake, we saw three non-psycho moose, a unique reddish colored black bear, and we didn't sink. It was a good day.

I dropped Al and our gear by the truck, then returned the boat to its hiding place, though I thought the risk of theft seemed low.

As I returned to the opening where we'd parked, Al was bent down picking up the last of our gear, but by feel rather than sight. His head was up looking intently at the last spot we'd seen the moose. He was ten feet away, his back to me, his focus straight ahead and intense.

"ERR," I said.

His hip surgery must have worked well because I hadn't seen that kind of athleticism from Al in a long, long time.

Homing in on Chukars

I saw my first chukar on a hillside. Okay, on a terrifying precipice above the Snake River back when Southeast Washington had a special early season for these exasperating immigrants.

Before that day, most of my bird hunting had taken place vicariously in the pages of outdoor magazines. In real life, I'd shot a handful of ruffed grouse, a pheasant, and had missed two ducks, but mostly I'd hunted deer and, with my hounds and a couple of buddies, raccoons. When my freshman college roommate Mike and I hitchhiked from our dorm in Pullman, Washington to the breaks of the Snake River in Wawawai Canyon to look for chukars, we found more than we expected.

Mike and I both grew up three hundred miles away in Western Washington. If you've ever seen a movie with a Washington setting, it's most likely been portrayed on film as constantly dark and rainy. There is a kernel of truth in that. The west side of Wahington has its share of beautiful sunny summer and fall days, but during hunting seasons, we'd spent more time among big trees, shadows, ferns, and rain than dry and warm. Neither of us had seen anything like the canyon country on the Washington-Idaho border. It was a revelation.

It was so big, and aggressively bright. From a ridgetop on that first day in chukar country, we could see three states but could barely find a patch of shade because, except in the draws, even the tallest sagebrush didn't reach the middle of my thigh.

We didn't have a dog. We didn't even have a car, and didn't have much of a plan of where to go; but with chukars, attitude and toughness…and youth, helped compensate for our impressive lack of knowledge.

I did not kill a chukar that day, and neither did Mike; but we each started the day with an unopened box of No. 6s. Fifty rounds between us. By the time we had our thumbs out for a ride back to campus, we had shot forty-nine of those shells. We were sore-footed, sunburned, thirsty, and fired up for the next time.

There were a lot of chukars in the Snake River Breaks in the early '70s. Eventually some of the unlucky ones began to stray into our shot patterns. We made up for poor shooting and overall ineptitude with enthusiasm and the body fat ratio of athletic teenagers. Before long, the alluring scent of cubes of chukar breast and melted butter sizzling in a mess kit fry pan on an unsanctioned one-burner hotplate regularly wafted down the dorm corridor from our room. It always drew a crowd.

In the decades since Mike and I were first entranced by chukars, I learned a few things. One of the lessons that helped decrease my steps-to-shot ratio was to ask for advice.

Chukar hunters are a small segment of the upland bird hunting community. While polite company may try to avoid eye contact with us, other chukar chasers feel a kinship and, while they won't share their spots, many are open to sharing insights.

I was fortunate to run into Jeff, a fellow chukar enthusiast who, when he's on flat ground, works for the Washington State Department of Fish and Wildlife as a biologist. Besides his passion for birds, he has the academic and research background to give his comments added, and earned, credibility.

Applying my own on the ground experience as well as Jeff's generous answers to my questions, I have been able to focus more on the fraction of a mountain most likely to host chukars.

Also, since that first chukar hunt, I've evolved. I have a vehicle now, a couple actually. I drive the old brush-scraped one in chukar country. I switched out my long barreled 12-gauge, full-choke pump for a prettier and lighter 20 side-by-side, and, of course, chukar hunting, and everything else, is better with a dog.

My first bird dog, Juice, was a yellow Lab. I got her from a friend of a friend. She was beautiful, almost white, and a wonderful companion; but in retrospect, she just didn't come from great hunting stock. She found me a few pheasants and enthusiastically retrieved wigeon and teal, but she and I rarely hunted chukars. She stuck too close and wore out too fast. Her first chukar was the easiest one I've ever gotten. We were still in modified choke range from the truck when she flushed a pair, and I knocked one down. Both of those events were frustratingly rare in those days. I drive by that spot frequently but never without a thought about Juice, my first chukar dog.

After Juice, I got Archie. Arch, a Cesky Fousek, came from an organization that takes their dogs and breeding seriously. I had to pass a rigorous "pre-adoption" screening process. Glenn, the guy who owned Archie's mother, was tough; he wouldn't send those pups home with just anyone. Arch at six weeks old was only available because Glenn had rejected multiple prospective buyers. I guess I interviewed okay, and I think I also got a boost because the pups were approaching the age where Glenn, his wife Lila, and Cera, the pup's mom, were feeling puppy fatigue and ready to see them go. A few weeks later, my wife, my thirteen-year-old daughter, and twin nine-year-old boys joined me on a drive to Montana where we picked up our new family member. The back seat of a Suburban stuffed with three kids and a ten-week-old bird dog puppy was a busy and very happy place. The beginning of something really good.

I was lucky the way it came about, and forever grateful that it did. Getting Archie changed everything.

Chukar country was just as steep as ever, and it was still either frying or freezing, but now I could walk 7 miles and cover 25. I had never seen anything like it. Archie was the canine equivalent of a hovercraft. He'd sweep the country, seemingly drifting just above it, and find me birds. Find us birds, we were partners. This was how it was supposed to be.

Sometimes his pace would slow, and he'd creep into a point. The next time Arch would bang into a wall of scent that slammed him to a stop as though he'd hit a screen door. Better yet, when I did my part, he'd find the birds I shot. With Arch I became a chukar hunter.

The more I hunt chukars, the more I find to like. There is beauty in the stark range these birds inhabit that is often imperceptible to the uninitiated. A cock pheasant at a distance is a noisy brown bird, but in your hand the kaleidoscope of colors and shapes is mesmerizing. Like that rooster, a close-up look is enlightening. There may be more subtle hues in the high desert than in a forest, but it's the magnitude of the vistas that overwhelm. A single sagebrush exhibits multiple shades and shadows. Chukar country is an acquired taste. I think it takes immersion not just observation to appreciate it. It may be more appropriate to say we earn the clarity to recognize the allure.

Last winter I was joined by a first-time chukar hunter. We were birdless when we scraped snow from a big rock and sat to eat a sandwich. He grinned and said, "This is so cool. I've never seen so many bull elk or mule deer bucks in a day, heck even a year."

I was so glad he appreciated those elk and deer. We'll often find bighorns and coyotes, too. Badgers, wild horses, I've even seen a cougar while chukar hunting.

It's not just about the birds. Chukar hunters walk and stumble through a landscape full of wildlife and vistas impossible to find near pavement.

One of the best things about my favorite bird, though, is access. A chukar hunter rarely has to knock on a rancher's door. Chukars don't choose to live among people and agriculture.

Though finding a place to hunt is easier than with other upland birds, actually finding chukars in that colossal landscape can be a challenge. When Mike and I wandered up that first chukar hill way back when, we just climbed and stumbled around until we found birds. Even with the freakish density of birds in those days, it took longer than it should have, but eventually we started to recognize subtle similarities in the places we got shooting.

Where chukars live, water means everything. Even a small seep transforms a hill. In a dry landscape, green attracts life, all kinds of life. Though they like and sometimes need it, I think chukars sense the danger in hanging around water sources. Their "in and out" policy is a behavior that evolved from predators hunting at those same waterholes since the first chukar deposited in North America strode across a parched slope.

I have found birds quite close to water, but more often I find tracks. The sight of tracks in the mud have often encouraged me to hunt harder, just knowing they're nearby. The birds go to water, but they don't live there; they are in the neighborhood though. There is no sure thing when hunting wild chukars, but a good bet is the area surrounding a green, wet spot, a mile or more from the next one.

Chukars get moisture from the bugs and vegetation they eat, but they do like an occasional drink. They also thrive on the insects that are dependent on the shady, moist micro-ecosystem of the spring or seep.

With moisture nearby, a hillside with cheatgrass and Sandberg's bluegrass is a good place to start looking for chukars. That same hillside with a rocky parapet is even better.

I've pondered the question of why chukars like to hang out in and around rocks. Apparently it's not just to twist hunters' ankles. Jeff suggested that one of the reasons is simply because it's good escape cover. Having spent time navigating those rocks, I'm sure he's right. In the rocks, it's easier for a chukar to gain the extra step or two on a bobcat or coyote so it can get airborne and whip down the mountain to safety.

Speaking of "down the mountain," the old saying that chukars run uphill, then fly down is back-breakingly true. The good news is that after the flush, when they accelerate toward the canyon bottom, they often wind around the lower end of the hogback and regain some or all of altitude they forfeited. Many times, I've watched a covey loop out of sight, made a mental note of the elevation, then reflushed them a draw or two over, much farther up the slope than I expected. This seems especially true when the original flush came after chasing the covey uphill.

Wind is a constant for chukar hunters. It makes the shots more difficult, and swirls scent so much, I've seen Arch and his successors lock up solid with the birds directly in back of them. When you walk in on a point, it's best to be ready for a flush from any direction. Wind can be an ally as well as a hindrance. When it's not just wind but *wind*, the birds are aware of the dips and swales that will give them cover. In a chukar hill gale, never pass a protected pocket.

Wherever chukars live, sagebrush is nearby. Open rocky, grassy areas are what most associate with chukars, but there are times when sagebrush might be your go-to cover. We all—hunters, chukars, and dogs—need a little shade in the early season. Chukars don't like trees, but sagebrush can give them respite from the sun. Later, though, in the cold and snow is when your hunt might be saved by adding a little sage.

This is another area where Jeff's advice really helped. Not only does the brush provide a bit of a windbreak, he told me, but with no bugs, and most of the seeds gone, grass is a staple. A bird that has to scratch to find grass appreciates a quarter-inch skiff of powder under the protective cover of sagebrush to the six-inch crusty blanket of snow outside. Chukar tracks dotting the snow in a line toward a patch of waist-high sagebrush isn't as good as a point, but it has great potential.

Dogs figure it out, too.

Archie had been out of my sight for a minute or two when I found chukar tracks new and sharp in the snow. I followed them over a small rise. When I crested the ridge, I spotted Arch straddling the tracks. He was leaning into the scent so hard I was surprised he didn't fall over on his nose. He was in the open pointing into a patch of sagebrush.

As I approached, I noticed a couple of tracks had veered off. Visually following along their path, I could see two chukars hunkered under their sagebrush sanctuary. I didn't know if the erratic breeze had Arch pointing the wrong way, or if I was looking at different birds. It didn't matter, because the pair I saw realized they were exposed and took off. That was enough to bust the rest of the covey, which Archie was handling perfectly. I swiveled to see both the covey and the pair, missed twice on the initial flush, and was still able to reload in time to miss a third shot at a straggler.

Arch was classy; he gave me a quick look, maybe shook his head, then went back to work.

Tracks in the snow, good advice, waterholes, rocks, swaths of cheatgrass, or just strong legs and a good attitude…all will help you find chukars. And the good news is, even when you get skunked, you got to be there.

Thursday Bucks

Big deer captivate me.

When I crawl through snow covered sagebrush on my belly to peek over a hogback into the next Montana draw, my anticipation is exhilarating. I hope, no I fully expect, to see a mule deer buck with heavy, long tined antlers which easily span that magical 30-inch standard. Symmetry in antlers is impressive, but I love a rack with wrinkles, odd angles, and sticker points. If things really go well, there will be drop tines.

That, in my entire life, I have never seen a buck like that—except in the travelling antler porn displays at Sportsman's shows—is an occasional annoyance, but next year I'll peek into other snowy arroyos, with unflagging faith, and another chance. I am confident that one day persistence and effort will collude to allow me to intersect in space and time with that outlandish buck. Until then I'll keep looking and enjoy the great, though somewhat smaller, bucks those Montana badlands do show me.

I know plenty of hunters who eagerly tell me they prefer "a nice meat buck to a tough old deer" or worse, "You can't eat antlers, you know." People who say these things should not be trusted in other matters either.

Big racks have an allure that cannot be denied.

I began deer hunting with my dad before Neil Armstrong put those first boot tracks on the moon. In those days, my goal was to see a deer, any deer in the wet part of Washington where we hunted blacktails. We usually did see a doe or two each October but, in my first few hunting seasons, I saw exactly as many leprechauns, unicorns, and sasquatches as bucks.

The fall of my senior year in high school, I got a buck. It was the last day of the season, the annual doe day. That was fortunate because the deer I took home was a bald buck fawn not appreciably bigger than my dog, but the drought, I hoped, I believed, was over.

I had been keen on hunting before, but actually tagging a deer ratcheted my zeal to a new level. This was just the start. Next season, I just knew, would be even better. I focused on enhancing my skills as a hunter. I read everything I could find, practiced with my rifle, scouted, learned to use binoculars. My effort paid off. I became one of those guys, the ones who get their deer.

That button buck began a string of years where I was able to find a legal deer during the rifle season. "Legal" being the bar that must be cleared to be considered a trophy in those days.

A few years later, done with school and somewhat gainfully employed, a buddy and I discovered that going places with more game and fewer trees made us better hunters. My first trip to Wyoming for mule deer and pronghorns was a revelation.

Prior to that Cowboy State trip, I'd been conditioned to believe that passing up a shot at a legal deer was akin to spitting in the face of the hunting gods. Dangerous foolishness verging on arrogance. It was like going for it on 4th down, with thirty yards to go, from your own ten. Potentially great reward, sure, but fraught with peril.

On those eastern Wyoming prairies, I could almost always spot pronghorns if I tried, and each wrinkle in the landscape seemed to hold mule deer. Several of those deer had antlers that forked—some forked more than once!

It was as though I'd been transported to the pages of the magazines I read and reread. I was practically Jack O' freakin' Conner!

In those books and magazines, discerning hunters would calmly size up a buck or a bull, then cooly decide to look for something bigger. Intellectually I understood the concept, but between understanding and truly believing was a gap as wide as those game-filled prairies; one that, until now, I didn't really believe could be bridged.

I did uneasily hold my fire for a day or two, nearly to the bursting point. My patience and selectivity were rewarded with a 13-inch pronghorn and a 2-point mule deer that trip.

On those sunny grasslands near Lander, Wyoming, I surrendered to the allure of antlers and horns. I was, apparently, a trophy hunter.

My status as a TH has led me to places where my resolve to hold out for a big one has been tested. I've often…usually, been found wanting.

For the past several years, my sons, Jake and Riley, and I have travelled to pursue mule deer on public land and block management areas in Montana. Coordinating three work schedules with season dates and WSU Cougar home football games slid us into a comfortable rhythm of hunting Saturday (on bye weekends) or Sunday through a half day on the following Friday before starting the long drive home.

A universal truth among us trophy hunters is you'll never get a really big buck if you hang your tag on a smaller deer. We wait until we encounter that super buck, the kind of buck where, when bewildering numbers are mentioned, they sound more like bowling scores than a reference to antlers. So I hike, glass, and keep seeking that calendar buck.

I hunt hard and won't shoot until I find a giant buck—unless, of course, I see a somewhat grown-up male deer…or Thursday, whichever comes first.

It is not uncommon by Wednesday for me to be second guessing my Sunday or Monday choices. Sometimes, depending on the weather, non-shooter's remorse kicks in as early as Monday evening.

Lying in my motel bed, I'm taunted by visions of giant racks I haven't seen and shots not taken at bucks I have.

These trips with my boys provide me with a year to dream about sharing with them that eventual meeting with a drop tine bruiser, a week of stories and fun, and venison. The anticipation and fun are a given—venison, the variable.

I finally drift off, comforted by the change in attitude the waning week engenders. Tomorrow will be the day.

Last year, late in the week, I almost got lucky. At first light on a narrow piece of state land, a long way out, we glassed what was clearly a first day buck. Four long points on a side, with a couple of feet of icy cold Montana air between the antler tips.

The stalk was a longshot from the start. It played out like those situations often do. The back of the knob I chose to circumnavigate for cover stretched much farther than I'd guessed. By the time I reached the vantage point I'd selected, the buck was gone.

A bit later, back at the truck, I informed Jake and Ri that I was done hunting. Now, "I am going to make meat."

I don't remember where I first heard the reference to making meat, but it resonated with me. I was a primal hunter now, like a caveman, or a lion. I was hunting to eat…and, it was Thursday.

The guys dropped me at the north end of a patch of BLM land a mile wide with a full two miles to the south before the fence designating private land beyond.

As the guys drove off to chase sharptails, their buck tags already filled, I contemplated the landscape. Gazing south from the frozen roadside, it appeared to be flat as a tabletop, and endless. It was covered with snow, sagebrush, and, as far as I could see, not a single tree.

Walking revealed its nature. What appeared to be a mesa was carved by cuts and draws, a furrowed field on a gargantuan scale. Each coulee a likely prospect, another draw just ahead.

This day most were empty, though one did hold a buck, a nice one. He busted me coming, too upright, over the top and bounced away. He was 4x3. Beautiful, brown rather than gray against the snow. He uncharacteristically stopped close enough for a rare offhand shot, but skylined. He contemplated me longer than I expected, then turned. I watched him go. Tentative steps before one, two, three bounces, his antlers the only thing visible on the last bound, then gone.

The next buck I spotted before he saw me. Rather than coming over the top, I'd crept to the crest of a hump in the mouth of a draw where it widened to a frozen creek bottom. Two deer were bedded on a sidehill in easy range. I ducked back out of sight, slipped my pack from my shoulders, then elbowed my way through the stunted, snow-sluffing sage to a spot where I could settle my elbows for a steady rest.

Both deer snapped toward my clumsy belly crawl. They rose nervously from their beds; each took a couple stiff-legged steps, then hesitated. At my shot, the doe stotted up the hill. The buck sprinted down and out of sight around a bend in the coulee.

I retrieved my pack, removed the snow that had accumulated in my pants during my snake-like sneak, and walked to the bed the buck had so recently vacated. The track was easy but unnecessary. I could see him, lying among the frosted sage, as though he'd tucked in by design rather than the randomness of the sudden system failure that ended his last run.

I approached carefully, made certain it was over, then sat by him in the snow.

I tucked a sprig of sage in the corner of his mouth—a tradition my dad taught me. I have no idea where Dad ran into this ritual of respect, but I understand it's an artifact of German and Austrian hunting. I have approached my sons sitting with deer they've killed to see that last bite in place. I wish Dad were still here to see that. Though I know of no German heritage in our family tree, we have appropriated this custom as our own. Those quiet, solitary moments after the deed is done deserve contemplation.

I stroked this deer's fine warm hide, then lifted his head to admire his antlers. By far the smallest Montana deer to ever wear my tag.

Despite the facetiousness of my claim to being a trophy hunter, I do like antlers, the bigger the better.

In the decades since that first Wyoming antelope, some pretty antlers have joined that pronghorn on my wall. I have two mule deer mounts with the capacity to make me react like my dog hitting a wall of pheasant scent. I'll slam into a point and gawk at the deep forks, the massive girth at the base, and the stunning width. Though neither meet the minimum standard of "the book," they rank near the top in my alternative, personal scoring system.

Looking at them kindles memories of the harsh cold in one instance, debilitating, attitude-sucking heat in the other. Both conjure the smiles, the voices of companions on those hunts, now scouting different realms.

This Montana buck won't make it to my wall, at least in the house. His youthful antlers atop a shining white skull hang with other modest but memorable headgear in my garage, near the freezer that contains a diminishing pile of two-person white paper packages emblazoned with magic marker proclaiming "Deer-Montana 2019."

I lumbered up from my snowy seat by the buck, then climbed out of the draw in search of good cell reception where I called the nearest of my deer hauling sons.

With Riley holding a leg, and me a knife, we completed the familiar process of converting this lately vibrant animal into an easy-to-drag collection of future meals and headed for the truck.

I drug the deer a while, then supervised the rest of the way. Ri needed no help, but I wanted a photo and besides, the process has many parts, skipping any is not an option.

While we have never seen a really big buck in the area we've made "our spot," Riley, Jake, and I have killed some pretty bucks on these Montana trips. A couple have been easy; some have required long hikes and seemingly longer drags just to reach a spot where we shouldn't have risked driving, but did. Each has a story, and each is memorialized on a wrinkled BLM map with an x, an initial, and two digits representing the year.

Neither the story nor the antlers of this buck are notable, yet I find myself reminiscing about this one more than many of his larger predecessors.

I recall intricate details of the frosty November prairie, beauty camouflaged by apparent monotony.

A solitary sharptail tilting his head, watching me, deciding how close an approach to allow, quick, close to his body wing movements as he struggled for balance against the wind that tried to push him off an angled piece of barbed wire stretched between broken, fallen wooden fenceposts.

The 4x3 that paused when he somehow sensed I wouldn't shoot while he was skylined.

Finally, after the anticipation of many days and likely draws, the deer, the denouement. A buck I would have enjoyed watching bounce away, unmolested, twenty-four hours earlier, meeting me on a cold Thursday afternoon.

Comes a Kudu

I nocked an arrow, then slightly bent my knees to get a better shooting angle through the skinny opening in the wall of our blind as two kudu bulls approached the water hole. We'd seen others, but this was different. Our Bushman guide Hans, and my wife Laurie, could feel it. They faded toward the dirt walls of the sunken blind to give me room to draw my bow. Though the bull I wanted was in range, standing broadside, I hesitated. I'd been warned that the shoulder blade was bigger than I, a deer and elk hunter, would expect. It had been drilled into me to hold out for the quartering away shot which would open a path for my arrow to slip behind that protective slab of bone on its way to the heart and lungs.

The bull turned slightly, took a step, then, before I had time to think, my familiar yellow and white fletching disappeared into buff colored hair near the bottom of a faint, vertical, off-white stripe—exactly as I'd pictured it during the months of practice in my yard.

A short, frantic run took both bulls out of sight, behind a curtain of brush and dust, but I had never been more certain of shot placement in my life.

Being in this place, climbing out of a partially underground blind to track a kudu across the sandy western edge of the Kalahari Desert, had not been remotely on my radar a few months prior when an email exchange with Don, a Montana friend, took a serendipitous turn.

"You know," I typed, "with the changes to the regs and the competition for non-res elk tags in Montana getting tougher, I think I'll go to BC. Instead of elk, I'll hunt grouse and catch trout this September."

Don must have recognized the frustration in my electronic comment. He responded a few hours later with, "Since you don't yet have firm plans for the fall, why don't you and Laurie join me and my wife in Africa?"

What? Africa? Why, that's…that's crazy talk.

Sure, I'd thought about Africa, every hunter has, but I hadn't really considered it. I'd read Hemingway and Ruark and admired exotic looking African animals poking out from the walls of sporting goods stores, but travel that far to bow hunt?

Didn't sound like me.

I'm really glad that invitation was in an email rather than on the phone. On a call, with no time to let it simmer, I probably would have declined. With the evening to mull it over and a discussion with Laurie, who is a real good sport, the allure of a safari began to invade my thoughts and erode my resistance. Eventually going to Africa didn't seem so outlandish after all. There was also that somewhat familiar gray-haired guy in the mirror asking, "If not now…when?" All night that hackneyed, but reasonable, question stubbornly replayed in my mind like a mantra.

That March morning, I couldn't have pointed out Namibia on a map. By noon the next day, Laur and I had booked our flights.

In late-August, after two long flights and a layover, Laurie and I stretched our legs and squinted in the bright African sunlight glistening on the tarmac at Windhoek International. There, along with our friends and a father son duo we'd just met, we connected with our hosts Allan and Jacqui Cilliers for the scenic drive north to their Sandveld Game Ranch.

A get acquainted cocktail hour at the lodge, a dinner featuring eland as the main course, followed by wide ranging conversation around the fire pit as night fell, set the perfect tone to consecrate our transition from jet age travelers to elemental archers.

Stories had slowed and the fire ebbed to glowing coals when we reluctantly said our goodnights, then we strolled the narrow cobblestone path to our secluded cottage. Laurie and I stopped partway to appreciate the stillness under a tiny sliver of moon whose minimal glow seemed to accent rather than interfere with our ability to marvel at the unfamiliar night sky garnished with stars we'd never seen.

Despite time zone-eating flights, and the long drive from the airport, it was easy to wake up early my first morning in Africa. Serenaded by birds speaking languages I'd never heard, I left Laurie to finish preparing for the day, then retraced my steps of the previous evening. As the pink bloom on the eastern horizon encroached on the fading stars, just steps from our cottage I stopped cold. Seeing a giraffe before my first cup of coffee was something I had neither anticipated nor considered, yet there he stood. In moments he sauntered into the bush, his unique rocking gait hustling him into cover that didn't seem tall enough or dense enough to hide him, but it did.

There were more and closer encounters with giraffes over the next week, but that first rendezvous was a defining moment for me. It made real that I was nearly as far from my home as is possible on Earth, nearly halfway around the world. I was reminded of the scene in the initial Jurassic Park film when they first encounter living dinosaurs. The power of the word "awesome" has been sapped, drained by overuse, but true awe is what I felt in that moment.

Africa was new to me, as fresh and unfamiliar as hunting from a blind. I grew up sneaking up—or, more often, trying to sneak up—on elk or blacktail deer on the soggy side of Washington state. Here, it hadn't rained in months, and there were birds as tall as elk.

Also, I've always liked to wander. Other than about an hour in a treestand, the only hunting I'd ever done from a blind was for waterfowl. I wasn't sure how I'd like it. I was even less confident that Laurie would be interested in or even willing to sit partway underground for hours at a time for the duration of our trip.

It was wasted worry. Even if the animals I'd come for never offered a shot, the number and variety of birds and mammals drawn to the water kept us enthralled. Despite not speaking each other's language, Hans instantly picked up on our interest in birds, as well as game animals, so he enthusiastically joined in the search for new specimens.

Years of hunting with a recurve bow has taught me to manage expectations. As I settled into the blind that first morning, I was hopeful, optimistic, but guardedly so. I wasn't counting on it, but with several species on my "would like" list, I thought it was at least a coin toss that a set of African horns—spiral, lyre-shaped, or straight—were destined for my wall. Not knowing what animals might show up kept me eagerly scanning the edges of the brush.

Shortly into our first morning, I was enjoying watching the busy antics of a particularly appealing Crimson Breasted Shrike hopping nearby when Hans whispered, "Comes a kudu." He stared at a spot to the right of the blind, then indicated where with the slow, minimal movement of just one finger.

I pride myself on having a good game eye. There is even some risk that I might get cocky while pointing out deer and elk back home.

I could not see that kudu.

After several minutes of Hans maintaining his gaze and pointing, I began to wonder if he was hazing me. Finally, through the brush, I was able to make out a fist-sized patch of hair on the withers of a young kudu bull. He was close, on the edge of recurve range. Even knowing where he stood, when I looked away, reacquiring that tiny piece of kudu hide through the foliage and thorns took a while.

The vegetation in the Sandveld is deceiving. It's not hard to traverse but surprisingly difficult to see through. Despite the annual months long dry spell, grass, though straw colored, with no hint of green, remained more than knee high. Trees and bushes are close and cross hatched, some with naked branches while others still carried a load of green leaves. The mix creates a pattern of shadows, sunlight, and cover that confounded me.

In the open, zebras, gemsbok, kudu, wildebeest, impala, and eland are striking. The stripes, horns, shapes, and coloring of each is unique, distinct from any of the others. Considering the obvious differences in appearance, it's baffling, and humbling, that they can all be so darn hard to see. Each of the diverse patterns and hues is surprisingly effective camouflage.

My ability to pick out visitors to the water holes improved as the days passed, but our time there was insufficient for me to even approach good.

Hans was a constant, thoroughly pleasant, reminder of the gap between my spotting ability and his.

Despite my steadfast hovering near one of the narrow shooting and spotting slots in the blinds, his whispered cue that an animal was nearby, or the slight back and forth movement of his index finger, a raised eyebrow, and a tilt of his head indicating direction almost always came before I suspected something was approaching.

The next morning began with Hans removing a poisonous snake from our blind. That pit viper, fresh leopard tracks circling the blind, and an impressive mound of rhino poop nearby, changed and charged the intensity of the day. It seemed prophetic.

After getting a feel for the land and the game, I became more a hunter, less an observer. I belonged here.

When, just before noon, that bull kudu offered the angle I needed, it felt preordained.

I was surprised in the aftermath of the shot. Even with a clearly lethal hit, I've always waited to begin a track. That is not the custom in the Kalahari. Apparently with leopards, hyenas, jackals, and the occasional lion roaming the landscape, injured or dead ungulates are not ignored for long. A quick follow up is intended to prevent meat loss, or an unpleasant dispute over ownership of a carcass. Hans waved me on, and we took up the kudu's trail within minutes.

Though the track wasn't long, I got a taste of the legendary tracking ability of the bushmen. I don't know what Hans saw or intuited, but, like the spotting of game, I was the weak link. I started slowly, looking for blood soaking into the sand. I was not seeing much. When I looked up, Hans had his hands clasped behind his back and was strolling across the tracked-up sand at a normal walking pace. He was looking ahead, not at the ground like me.

Blood disappeared into the sand almost instantly and, from my perspective, there was no way to tell one hoof print from the hundreds of others, yet we walked up on the bull as though Hans knew where he would go and just went to that spot.

When I first saw the bull cautiously ease toward the water, I knew I'd take the shot if I got the appropriate bearing. After that I tried to ignore those dramatic horns to maintain focus on the vital spot for my arrow.

I'm glad I did. The shot was as true as it had seemed, and there was no ground shrinkage.

The bull had not gone far. He was not the biggest of his kind, but the thick, dark spirals extended farther up and out than in the image burned into my memory. Despite my confidence in the shot, I was relieved and grateful for the short track.

After checking with Hans to verify I had the appropriate vegetation, I gave the bull his last bite. Laurie, Hans, and I admired the kudu, then took the obligatory photos. I was struck by how the elegant curves of his horns evoked a slightly distorted echo of the shape of my recurve.

When Allan, summoned by radio, arrived, everything happened quickly; More efficiently than I'd ever experienced.

Allan was able to drive to within the length of his available cable from where the kudu fell. In a surprisingly short time, he and Hans winched my elk-sized bull, whole, onto the bed of a Land Rover for the return to camp.

I remember elk, moose, deer, even pronghorns that required a lot of hunched over knife work, grueling backpacking, and sometimes, if I was lucky, horses or llamas. More than once, as I strained under a pack, I fervently wished for an easy way out of the tough job of getting heavy loads of meat to a road.

Seeing that bull drug into a truck was bittersweet. Packing big game is hard work, so I appreciated the ease of the process, though it felt as though I'd left something undone. My hands were unbloodied, the familiar scents missing.

Thinking about the field care of the meat, and horns, in the months since, I came to accept that it was exactly the right thing to do. Taking the bull to the field dressing station at the lodge was an efficient and incredibly clean process. I wasn't able to bring home any meat, but I got to see that every bit was used and appreciated.

In the weeks prior to this trip, I wavered about hunting from a blind. I have always liked to see what was over the next hill, and stalking thrills me. I wasn't sure about waiting and watching. On that count, I have no ambivalence. The abundance, variety, and proximity of wildlife made hours and days in the blinds great fun and too short.

Like spring bear hunting, we started each day early but didn't need to be hunkered in our hides at first light. We'd spend the morning hours in a blind, retreat to the lodge for lunch and a stretch, then return to our morning set up, or try a new spot with better wind conditions to watch until sunset.

Each morning Hans, Laurie, and I witnessed the awakening of the Kalahari from atop the cab high seat in the open back of a Land Rover. Every evening, we rode back to the lodge in the same seat during the unvaryingly red dusk. Both ways watching for birds, game, and dodging overhanging branches.

One evening we, okay Hans, heard the somewhat goose-like sound of zebras in the distance. They seemed to be coming our way. With a hand-held radio, Hans alerted Allan to postpone our normal sunset pick up. I'm not sure what was different that night—maybe it was because we'd become so comfortable here but could feel our time slipping away. It might have been the combination of sights and sounds so new yet so…right. But it was special.

The zebras came in single file. They barked and splashed in the shallow water just yards from our elevated blind. As the colts kicked and bucked, and the adults shouldered their way to the best spots, I got a little misty. When I looked at Laurie, there were tears on her cheeks.

The zebras were unaware of us but kudus, down-wind, coughed unheeded warnings. We stayed until full dark that night.

Despite a lifetime of wandering with my bow, and my anxiety about being bored in a blind, it was wonderful. Laurie and

I included novels as well as an invaluable bird identification book in our daypacks. We did read a little, but I was surprised and pleased at the small number and short duration of those times.

Bowhunters, particularly longbow and recurve archers, deal with much different range and shot placement constraints than rifle hunters. With blinds near water and oriented to take advantage of prevailing winds, our standard day provided multiple, archer friendly close encounters with game animals. Sometimes absurdly close. One morning, when an eland took a last look around before committing to bend down for a drink, Laurie, using the sound of his drinking as cover, whispered to me, "Look at those beautiful eyelashes."

With a lot of waterholes and only a handful of guests at any time, each morning and afternoon, discussion led to analysis about how the breeze would affect specific blinds and which animals were more likely to approach which waterhole. Like all hunting, even with Allan's decades of experience, it's always a guess as to what, if anything, will show up where or when.

Don has hunted in Africa many times. On this trip, other than photos, his single archery objective was a blue wildebeest, something that has eluded him. For him, on this trip, that chance never came. I'd decided upfront I wasn't going to take a wildebeest so, of course, two different bulls on different evenings came to my blind.

With my recurve, I came home with wonderful memories and the skull and horns of a fine kudu. I also blew a great opportunity at a gemsbok, and enjoyed close encounters with new and fascinating African birds, big game, and small mammals. I'd decided ahead of time that warthogs, zebras, duikers, eland, and those wildebeests would be allowed to pass unmolested. In retrospect, I slightly regret some of my choices. Only slightly though, because now I have a reason, a desire, and the beginning of a plan to return to the Kalahari.

Night

"Holy Cow, Run Away!"

My buddy Dwight, who was enthusiastically encouraging me to join him in retreat, and unwittingly paraphrasing Monty Python, may be the most gentle and pious man I've ever known, but the sudden screaming of a bull elk mere steps away compounded by darkness so complete we couldn't tell the sky from the trees, momentarily confounded his normal calm.

We'd parked my truck, then crept into the woods below the road for a midnight bugling session. We'd chased bulls around the adjacent wilderness area for a week, getting an occasional glimpse and hearing them bugle, but, so far, had been skunked. With just one morning left, we hoped to increase our odds with this late-night scouting mission. If a bull answered, we'd have a place to start in the morning.

We got our answer all right, and I did kill an elk there the next morning, before the dew dried. Not the bull though. A cow responded to our calls. I might have passed the shot earlier in the week; on our last day, I didn't hesitate.

I'm glad I got that cow, but my shining memory from that trip was not the close-up cow, the short track, or the freezer stuffed with venison; it was the late-night bull I never saw.

Many of my most vivid sporting life memories took place between dusk and dawn—making them hard to photograph, but impossible to forget.

It became Pavlovian for me to associate dark with fun from an early age.

Where I grew up, Canada geese were scarce when I was a kid. Seeing or hearing them was rare. I remember my dad excitedly waking me late one night so we could run outside to listen to geese conversing as they passed.

I stood on the cold cement of the driveway in my astronaut PJ's and bare feet, with my neck craned, face tilted toward the impenetrable night sky, gazing at the sound of the geese. I imagined them looking down from their invisible flight path and wished so hard that I could see them.

Geese made the night mysterious and full of possibility.

So did crawdads.

My folks bought a lake cabin when I was little. Rules were different at The Lake. There were shooting stars to see and campfires to poke. I got to stay up late, even later if I was on the dock catching crawdads.

A chicken bone, drumsticks worked best, on the end of a string was my crawdad rig. At first, I used a flashlight to watch the little lobsters move toward the bone, but later, as my crawdad catching skills grew, I preferred to just hold the string and feel the faint buzz in my fingertips when a crawdad began to haul away his prize. Once a crawdad, or sometimes two, claimed the bone, I'd slowly haul the string, hand over hand. I'd learned to never let the back of a crawdad break the surface or they'd let go. Lying prone on the dock, my ten-year-old arms were just long enough to reach under the crawdad by holding the end of the handle on the old tin pot my mom let me use for a "net."

It took a while for the bone to attract my prey. While waiting, bats would flash by above, even between us, darting black shadows against a slightly less black sky. Lying on a dark dock whispering with a buddy or just the background murmur of grownups talking while waiting for crawdads is a very good way for a boy to spend a summer evening.

Coon hunting seemed like a reasonable next step.

I got my first coonhound a month before I could drive. Jude was a plot-redbone cross. Sixteen years and a pack of hounds later, I gave up coon hunting to spend winter nights doing daddy stuff rather than coon hunting, but by then I was like a vampire. Hounds and raccoons made me a creature of the night forever.

As coon hunters, my buddies and I spent a lot of time in the woods at night. We wandered creek bottoms and beaches, listening to or looking for dogs. Regularly we sank ourselves, and once a truck, in beaver ponds and creeks. We crashed through nettles, froze our fingers and toes, climbed, and fell out of trees, dented and mired our parents' trucks, then later our own, and sometimes treed a coon.

Once, in the August no kill season, a friend and I took just one dog, my old Black and Tan, Judge, hunting along the Tahuya River. We hadn't seen Judge in a while, nor had he opened on a track. Eventually we caught up with him in a small clearing along the riverbank. He was chewing something. When I got my light on him, I could see he was shredding a brown paper bag of snacks. A few feet away lay a sleeping bag. The whimpering emanating from it was pitiful. A boy, on a family camping trip, had ramped up the adventure quotient. He was bivouacked on his own away from his folks' campsite near the road. The boy, certain this dark, snuffling, nightmare marauder was a bear, lay turtled and quaking in his sleeping bag awaiting the inevitable.

The kid was happy to see us. After a bit of eye wiping and deep breathing to compose himself, we walked with him to his family's tent.

Another time I was alone when I heard Judge treeing. He seemed to be a long way off; an instant later, he sounded much closer, then distant again. When I found him, he was bayed up in a hole under a slash pile. When he lunged inside, it created the illusion of distance. I hauled Judge back to get a better look. The gap under, and between logs, was a few inches wider than my shoulders and about twice that tall. I allowed myself a moment of rumination, then elbowed Judge aside and belly crawled into the hole. I had my .22 pistol in one hand and a flashlight in the other. Inching along with both arms stretched out front, I was excited. Judge and I had caught coons, but I'd convinced myself there was a bobcat down that hole. It would be our first.

As I slithered into that cavern, my perspective began to change. Even though the soles of my feet were probably still outside, mentally I was underground. I got a little queasy as I began to recognize just how snug the tunnel was. And it was getting tighter. Unpleasant visions of being stuck momentarily slowed my progress. Inching ahead that last foot, I had my shoulders hunched and, in order to look forward rather than straight into the dirt, I had to push my head hard against the top of the tiny, continuously shrinking shaft. My flashlight was weak, but I figured it wouldn't take much to reflect eyeshine, and I intended to put 40 grains into one of those bright spots.

Porcupines, it turns out, don't face you when they're cornered. When I realized that the unfamiliar sound I heard, during infrequent gaps in Judge's barking, was a tail full of quills snapping back and forth, it focused my attention. In the dim and fading light from my trusty 3 cell, I finally made out the lighter color of the business end of the porcupine, RIGHT THERE. My eagerness to back out of that hole cannot be overstated.

Judge, his resolve buoyed by my presence, really wanted to get by me and shake that porcupine. It got busy. I suggested to Judge that he back up. Since there was no room on either side, he responded by trying to climb over my head as I was scrambling to back out. Multiple times my face slammed into the ground, accelerated by 70 pounds of fired up, baying black and tan bouncing my head like an Olympic diver on a springboard. My increasingly stern instructions to Judge would end with a grunt and bits of bark and dirt in my mouth. People say that during car wrecks time seems to slow down. This was like that. Despite the noise and activity, I had time to ponder what would happen if the porcupine decided to make a run for it. Since I was blocking the only way in or out, I actively hoped the porky would just wait out my exit. That is just what happened. In a short while it all worked out with no lasting injuries to any of the parties involved. Judge was reluctant to leave though, and maintained a bad attitude about porcupines throughout his life.

Coonhunting is just one of many reasons to be in the woods at night.

Curley and I played high school football together. After a game, like most ballplayers, we'd be too keyed up to sleep. We'd attend the ritual post-game rehash at Pizza Pete's, then drop off our dates, link up with Bruce, the third member of our crew, and head for the hills.

One October night, we reached a trailhead with excess time and energy.

Even though our deer hunting destination was less than three miles up the trail with five hours before daylight, we headed out and up. Bruce had thought to bring a flashlight, so he led the way. Since he could see, he walked faster than Curley and me. Our stumbling and the occasional slap of a branch across the face was irritating.

"Bruce," we whined, "shine the light back sometimes, and slow down, we can't see."

He opined that we needed to "quit crying and keep up." He maintained his pace. A version of this bickering continued until Bruce had had enough. He had a pretty good arm. When he flung the flashlight, it spun through the black timber like a dust devil comprised of light rather than debris. The surreal pirouettes abruptly stopped with a metallic crunch against a fir.

After an extended moment of silence, Bruce said, "Now you can see just as good as me!"

We could.

Deer and elk hunting always seems to have a nighttime component.

My old friend Ronnie and I went on a sort of guided trip in the Little Belts in Montana. Before sun up, Floyd, our "guide," would drive us from the lodge to drop us at the head of various canyons where he thought we might find elk. He'd attend to other business during the day to return for us before dusk. It annoyed him that we were never back at the road waiting for him. We'd get to the trailhead thirty minutes, even an hour or more after shooting light to be scolded by Floyd about how "Good hunters are out of the woods before it gets dark!" It seemed to be his one rule, and he cared about it, a lot.

The last night of our hunt, Floyd had someone with him as he fumed about our tardy arrival. He'd piggybacked ranch chores with our shuttle and had brought along a young cowboy to take three horses down the mountain to the barn at the lodge. The plan was for the wrangler to ride one and lead two. There were several saddles in the back of Floyd's truck, so Ronnie and I stashed our bows in the back seat and volunteered to ride with the hired hand back to the ranch.

The "cowboy," it turned out, was a scared teenager who knew very little more about horses than we did. He was glad for the company. Ronnie and I, being just a few years older than our cowboy, agreed that two or three hours on horseback was a far better option for our last night than enduring a slow, winding 30 miles in a rattling old pickup on a washboard road accompanied by another harangue from Floyd.

It was glorious. The night was mild, the kind of moonless Montana September starlight that you don't just look at, you become part of. As we walked our horses down the berm-closed road, a meteorite flashed across the sky so big and close we could clearly see the wonder on each other's faces and the surrounding terrain in sharper detail than at noon. In the dark after the fireball passed, we were transformed. We were cowboys.

With our newfound confidence, we all sat taller in the saddle. Cowboys would get to the ranch way faster than a trio of dudes. We were riding a road, for crying out loud, not some hard to navigate mountain trail. It was time our horses understood who was in charge and, pleasant though this was, it was getting pretty late.

All we were missing were six shooters and appropriate hats.

A couple clicks of the tongue, a little squeeze with our heels, and we picked up the pace.

By acclamation, the horses passionately and unanimously agreed that getting back to the barn sooner was a fine idea. We never touched a trot as all three horses joyfully rocketed through the gears from saunter to stampede.

Galloping down the dark mountain two track, it became evident that the curves in the road were closer together than they had appeared mere moments before. Even so, I don't remember any screaming until the puddle. A couple things about a puddle: first, in the dark, anyone could mistake an innocent puddle for a giant hole. It was a revelation how much…anticipation one can conjure in the instant between seeing what appears to be a crater right where your speeding mount's next step will land, and the first splash. Second, after that infinitesimal fraction of a second of relief that it's water and not a crevasse, it crosses your mind—at least it did mine—that it might be deep.

It all worked out. The horses remained upright, we all stayed aboard, tenaciously if not gracefully, and subsequent puddles were less intimidating, but that night I swore off nighttime downhill horse racing.

A few years later, I took a first timer on a spring bear hunt in north Idaho. Late on the third day, I spotted a grazing black bear on a ridge just one canyon away.

When I pointed it out to Joe, he barely looked through his binoculars; he just jumped up and was ready to go.

"It's getting pretty late, Joe," I said. "That's a big drop, meaning a steep climb back up. Let's get him tomorrow."

"Let's get him now!" Joe blurted.

Well, if this greenhorn was good to go, then I certainly was.

The canyon between us and the bear was rougher, deeper, and even steeper than we'd expected. We were still a long way from the bear when we ran out of light. Luckily, during our stalk, we'd crossed a hiking trail. A trail, we decided, despite potential backtracking, would be easier than retracing our route, especially since—this being a recurring theme—neither of us had a flashlight.

It started as a nice enough path, but it was spring, in the mountains. Even in the dark, we made good time on the open south facing slopes where this medley of miserable choices began, but when we entered the timber, snow obliterated the trail. It was, after all, spring, in the mountains.

Cloudy nights under tall trees create a special kind of dark, and it was steep. I'd crab across angled snow, fingers and toes curled into the crusted, rotting slush to keep from sliding down the mountain. Once across, I'd probe with my boots for a level spot with slightly turned up edges. If that lasted a few steps, I'd deem it the trail and call for Joe to crawl over. Then we'd move to the next snowbank. It was slow going.

The last few miles were on a road, and by then it was day-light, so it was easy. Later, I checked a map. We walked 22 miles that night.

Trails in the dark, even really long ones, are easier than uneven ground you can't see, especially when packing meat.

John and I had hunted several days in SE Montana. We'd seen bucks better than either of us had ever taken, but they were all too easy. We agreed that we "hadn't driven 1,200 miles, through intermittent blizzards, to shoot a buck from the truck!" I finally shot a modest whitetail buck during a near white out snowstorm. We wanted a mule deer for John as our trip was winding down.

Late November days at that latitude don't last long, and lunch had been a while ago when John said, "There's my buck!" He pointed toward a two-point mule deer trimming bitterbrush about a quarter mile from where we stood. A couple of miles in back of us lay the road, and the truck.

It crossed my mind to point out how long a pack we were setting up but, as the guy with the filled tag, I kept that thought to myself; after all, this was "John's buck."

We snuck that deer. I found a vantage point while John went the last bit alone and got in close. By the time I arrived for the handshake, the sky was deep purple. In the fading light we got the buck dressed and sectioned into front and back pieces that would give us comparable loads.

It wasn't a big deer and, in those days, we both had dark hair and good knees. Still, it was half a deer on our backs, two to three miles across uneven ground, and I still hadn't yet learned to carry a flashlight. The cold was intense, my nose hairs sharp and stiff as needles, and, of course, it was dark. As we helped each other into our packs, it felt like the beginning of an ugly ordeal.

I never enjoyed packing a load like I did that buck. The pur-ple sky had long since ripened to black. The clouds had cleared, so moonlight on snow helped us pick stumble free routes. With waning light and not an extra inch of parachute cord, we'd somehow created two perfectly balanced packs. Coyotes sang their customary songs about John's buck, but more than the normal yipping and howling chorus, they created new verses as they chose to escort us all the way to the truck.

The song of those badlands coyotes that frigid Montana night and the sensation of well-being as we packed that deer remains with me, as do the individual voices of my hounds, the delicate clicking of crawdad claws in a tin pot, distant talk of migrating geese, and bugling elk, in tight or a ridge away. Like the smiles and laughter of old friends, unseen, unheard, yet vivid and indelible, enhanced by darkness.

Hunting in the Trad Zone

Growing up in the 1960s, my friends and I didn't have video games. We had no virtual reality, nor access to unlimited music or movies through seemingly magic electronics. We'd played outside until the streetlights came on. If we wanted to talk to someone outside of hollering range, we'd either walk to their house or go indoors to call on a rotary phone hanging, permanently and prominently, on a wall where everyone in the house could hear our conversation.

One thing that made life bearable in those dark times was TV—small, black and white TV. Once a week, except in the summer, my street light curfew assured that I would be indoors in time to see *The Twilight Zone*.

The stories were sometimes too subtle for me but always intrigued and entertained, often to the point of goosebumps.

One episode of *The Twilight Zone* hunkered down in my mind and has lived there ever since.

I don't remember any particular "aha" moment at the time, but that story stuck with me as firmly as a grouse arrow in the trunk of a fir tree, partly because the theme relates to traditional bowhunting.

A small-time hood was killed in a shootout with police. He awoke to find himself in a glorious afterlife. He enjoyed nothing but the best he could have imagined. In life he was a gambler, in death he still was—cards, dice…he bet big and won regularly. He had beautiful and accommodating feminine companions. His butler provided him with gourmet fare and the best liquor or champagne at his whim. His apartment was more luxurious than any he'd seen.

You can guess how this ends. A month went by, and he was bored. He told his butler he wanted to consider "the other place." As his smiling host gleefully pointed out, his initial assumption that he was in heaven was a tragic misreading of the situation.

Even as a kid, that wasn't too subtle for me.

There is no "gamble" without potential loss. No way to win if you can't lose. It's risk that provides the kick. His hell, his eternal punishment, was the certainty of winning.

While in most cases, traditional bowhunters don't face physical danger, the uncertainty of our quest is the allure.

We know before we head afield how tough it will be to get close enough to make our shot.

When we do manage to stalk within range, we haven't won, we've maybe reached the quarterfinals. We may earn the opportunity to shoot which—given shaky arms, erratic breathing, unseen twigs, the limitations of our equipment, and luck—can easily result in a miss. If we beat the odds on those initial obstacles, we still face the possibility of the pain, for hunter and prey, of a poor hit. When we do it all right, get close, make that perfect shot, there is still angst. From the moment the string slips from our fingers until we put our hands on our quarry, we wonder. "Was it enough?" "Did I see what I thought I saw?" Even our success is fraught with uncertainty.

This is clearly not a smart way to hunt.

There are other less demanding and emotionally draining ways to get antlers on the wall and venison in the pan.

Last week I saw an old friend; he told me about his recent purchase.

"This new bow is incredible," Scott told me. "I had low end compounds before. This bow cost a lot more, but it's worth it. It's a real game changer."

Though he allowed that the difference in accuracy he experienced might be partly because he has become more skilled, he was convinced the newer technology, better components, and tighter tolerances all contributed mightily to his shrinking groups and confidence to 60 yards, 70 yards, maybe even more.

"And," he said, his eyes sparkling, "there is discussion of allowing electronics on bows in Washington."

Confused, I asked, "What do you mean electronics? In what way?"

"Range finders built right into the sights so that when you lock on a deer the integral rangefinder calculates the distance, then the sight pin moves to the appropriate spot. You'd never have to use a separate rangefinder or estimate range!"

"Gee," I said "maybe someone will design a heat seeking arrow where all you have to do is launch it over a likely looking patch of cover so the arrow can detect and hit the deer, then send a GPS location when it dies."

Scott is a good hunter and a good sport, so he took my ribbing with a smile, but my comments, though meant to be facetious, carried more than a little…frustration, sadness, even nostalgia.

I have to be careful; I am not a purist. In my tech-related irritation, I'm aware there is the faint, maybe even pungent smell of hypocrisy.

For the last several years, early November finds me and my sons peering up sagebrush coulees in central Montana with rifles in our hands, my recurve 900 miles away hanging from an elk rack in my gear room.

I enjoy those trips with my sons as much as any hunting I do. With our rifles, we have a more communal hunt which is a big part of the fun and is more likely to generate venison.

I added hunting with a recurve to my rifle efforts as a teenager but switched to a compound for many years before going back to a recurve in the late 1990s.

My long time, jack of all hunting methods, master of none, along with my, to me, surprisingly long tenure as a hunter gives me perspective.

When I started bowhunting, tree stands were jerry-rigged plywood curiosities used, as far as I could tell from the magazines I read, by a few eccentric eastern deer hunters.

Range finders were something I'd expect to see on *The Jetsons* or *Star Trek*.

Eventually wheels, then cams on bows, came along to speed up the arrow while allowing the hunter to hold much less weight than he could ultimately unleash. Pure magic.

Impressive innovations all—certainly each increased the efficiency of tech savvy bowhunters.

When our predecessors laid down their spears and started flinging atlatl darts, I doubt there was a curmudgeon among them who scratched at his loincloth and railed against those "gol dang newfangled" gadgets.

If it meant the difference between eating or going hungry, I'd be happy to call in an air strike on an elk.

Efficiently killing game for most of human history has mattered a great deal, but is not why I, and many others, hunt with our recurves and longbows. Our methods are inefficient, but we won't starve if, at the end of the season, we have a leftover tag rather than a full freezer.

Venison is not the objective but a wonderful, and tasty, byproduct of the challenge. Difficulty and long odds the real, and peculiar, point.

I occasionally reminisce about a December morning in Southwest Washington that I shared with five bucks. Three of them 4 points. They were enjoying the sun on a south facing slope while my cold, camouflaged self watched from under a fir on the ridgeline just 50 yards above the nearest and biggest of the bunch. Periodically I'd slide backward on my belly down the off side of the hill until well out of sight, to stand, stretch, shiver from the cold a little, and wish I had a rifle, or at least a compound bow. I'd pace, shrug, and shake the tension from my neck and shoulders, then creep back to my hiding spot.

This watching and hoping routine consumed a good chunk of the morning. I finally cracked under the pressure of all those bucks so close. I decided to become invisible and slither within range. The wind may have shifted, or, it's possible my invisibility failed. Whatever the reason, shortly into my stalk, all five deer bounced down the open hillside toward the Klickitat River and out of my life.

I would have loved to have tagged the alpha of that pack of deer, or any one of the others. That was a long time ago, yet I remember it clearly.

Had I crested that hill with my rifle, or likely even a modern compound bow, that hunt would have abruptly ended with one of those bucks wearing my tag. I would still have those antlers to admire and would have shared the meat from that buck with family and friends.

The encounter with those deer would have lasted seconds to maybe a minute.

I spent at least two hours with them. I watched as they chewed their cud. I saw the puffs of steam from their nostrils backlit by the sun in the cold air. I also experienced the occasional sharp adrenaline spike when a repositioning buck gave me momentary hope for a shot.

I'm glad I had my recurve that day.

Another time I took a friend hunting during the rifle season. He'd never hunted and was enthusiastic about the process. We stopped to sit a while, so Tom was digging a snack from his pack when movement in some vine maples attracted my attention. I looked through my binocs: a buck! Unaware we were there.

"Tom," I whispered, "there's a buck, see? Below the big stump?"

I looked over the terrain between us and the deer, quickly analyzing the best route to close the gap.

"Let's sneak around this way," I said, pointing slightly downhill and indicating a route that would provide some cover.

Tom, the first timer, as pure a rookie as could be, looked at me, then quietly asked, "Why can't I shoot from here?"

I looked at the buck, about 80 yards away, nodded, said, "Yup, you could do that. Good idea."

He did.

Bowhunting will do that to you. Seeing game within reasonable rifle range is merely the opening act.

Closing the gap on a deer to which you've been psychically connected since first light then finally getting close enough to see the cud move in his throat, is time spent at an intensity level in a different realm than making a shot from a couple of hundred yards out.

Calling a randy, rutty bull to ten yards, rather than settling the crosshairs on him across a canyon, is not a morally or ethically superior act, and means nothing to the elk, but it is different and satisfying in a way that requires experience rather than words to truly understand.

Reflecting on what I said about perspective; I would have been heartbroken if the deer tag I didn't notch that morning

I spent with the five bucks was among the first I'd purchased. I don't pretend that all hunting is about "communing with nature," nor should it be. I encourage hunters to bag game—especially new hunters. Hunt during rifle seasons, take a doe when it's appropriate, build experience and, yes, perspective, while enjoying venison and hanging a bow or a hat on antlers that rekindle memories.

That hoodlum who thought he was in heaven had the best of everything and enjoyed it for a while. I don't blame him. Success at cards or hunting matters. That first deer or elk is a big deal, with a recurve, a compound, or a rifle. Then getting a big one, and consistently filling tags, wonderful.

Over time, it changes. Eventually, trying to understand the animals, how the wind moves relative to time and terrain, or passing a shot opportunity because…well, just because.

Embracing less efficient traditional gear and tactics to make hunting more difficult? That's turning evolution backward. It's like something from *The Twilight Zone*.

The Lagoon

"Was that the last time hunting the outside blind?" I asked Mark from the driver's seat of my old Tahoe.

The landscape rolled by as Mark hesitated just a little too long, then his answer was vague, non-committal. It felt like he was trying to let me down easy.

Several years back we stopped hunting the inside blind at Mark's home place in deference to the urban sensibilities of transient tenants in a nearby vacation rental. The outside blind had, until now, been far enough away to escape the tide of change that seems to engulf so many important places.

I've lost favorite spots to "progress" before. Recollections of great days and missing friends, human and canine, spread like ashes over the places where we made those memories; facing the loss of access to the Lagoon, while not the magnitude of a death, stoked a familiar melancholy. This is a special place, a resigned and sad goodbye.

My first time at the Lagoon was a revelation. I was the new guy in a boisterous quintet of twenty somethings. Well before the sky began to pink, we split into two groups, set decoys, drained green thermoses of coffee, then hunkered down behind the gray, weathered wood remains of blinds built by men who grew beards before they saw their first automobile. As I crouched in the dark listening to the same duck talk that drew those blind builders to this brackish tideland more than a hundred years ago, I was an outsider, unfamiliar with this shoreline-scented Oz, on the verge of being allowed a glimpse behind the curtain.

Shooting light and a flock of widgeon arrived simultaneously. As they homed in on our set, we instinctively coiled even lower. Mark whispered, "Wait…wait…NOW!"

Despite the size of the flock and the ruckus of my companions leaping to their feet, I locked in on one duck. With gray feet reaching for the water's surface, wings cupped, and neck arched to survey the landing zone, the first decoying duck I'd ever seen tried to reverse course. Then magically, it seemed at the time, he collided with my pattern.

There were two shells left in my Mossberg pump, but I was oblivious to the commotion. Unaware of the sound of wings, and my experienced companions banging away, it didn't occur to me to shoot again. I was focused on my beautiful drake. He floated on his back, kicked one leg three times, then stilled next to a tendril of seaweed.

When the shooting stopped, I waded out, gathered my duck and my wits, then hustled back to the blind. I was admiring where iridescent green met the cream top of his head when the next flock approached. This time green-winged teal. I was ready. I emptied my gun. Didn't touch a feather.

I went home with ducks that day. I don't remember how many. It was more than the one widgeon but fewer than the regs allowed. I do remember that I was jacked up.

Why had I not done this before? I'd had more shooting before noon than in all the deer and black bear hunting I'd done in my entire life.

Duck hunting was fun! I so hoped Mark would invite me back.

He did. The multi-generational impact of that invitation, and those that followed, has been remarkable.

That widgeon splashed in front of the outside blind forty years ago October. Last fall, in that same blind, I crouched again, watching ducks appear as dots on the horizon. This time I encouraged my grandkids to sit still, put their camo caps back on, or at least try to keep their bright blond heads below the top board, out of sight.

"Finn, Avery, hunker down until I stand to shoot. Make sure your earplugs are in tight!"

They didn't keep their heads down of course, but neither did their dad when he was their age. A reduced mortality rate among the ducks is a good trade in exchange for having kids at the Lagoon.

I didn't yet have a bird dog that first morning with Mark and his friends. I filled that gap the following year. Each of my dogs in the years since retrieved their first duck from the calm waters of the Lagoon. I always hoped the first few would be teal. Bigger ducks, especially mallards, but even widgeon, can intimidate eager but uncertain pups. All the dogs learned quickly though. By the time pintails arrived in December, October's tentative retrieves evolved into aggressive entries and confident chases.

Those low bank, early retrieves at the Lagoon were integral to building trust and confidence as those pups grew into fine hunters and better friends. Each spent many happy days there. All, from a vibrant eight-year-old killed in a fluke accident, to a cloudy eyed veteran of fifteen seasons, proudly handed me the final duck of their lifetimes on that grassy shoreline.

Four years ago, my current buddy, Colt, made his bravura Lagoon debut at eight months old. He didn't start with the teal I hoped for. Colt was baptized by a drake mallard. He hit the water unable to fly but could still swim. Colt closed the gap quickly. When the greenhead decided he couldn't outdistance Colt, he dove. Colt spun looking for the duck he knew was nearby. They were both surprised when the duck made the tactical error of surfacing close to Colt's muzzle. Colt grabbed him. The first timer held tight as the big duck kicked his feet while flapping one wing, turning the two of them in three full circles before a better grip put Colt in charge for good. When he delivered his prize to me, I thought it might just have been the best first retrieve ever.

I didn't expect then that it would be the last, first retrieve I'd see in the Lagoon, or that those bittersweet last retrieves had ended with Colt's grandpa Clancy.

My dad, like my dogs, got both his first and last duck at the Lagoon. Unlike my dogs, it was the only duck my dad ever got. That was the day we ran low on shells because my seventy-year-old dad, a lifelong rifle hunter but new to a shotgun, learned he had a dominant left eye and a lifetime of shooting righthanded.

My sons, Jake and Riley, like me, their grandpa, the dog whose hairy back they gripped with mini fists while taking their first steps, and all the dogs that followed, had their first up close encounters with ducks at the Lagoon as well. Also, like the dogs, and me, they spent a lot of time in that cold water.

The dogs swam to retrieve. The guys only needed a sibling near enough to the water to entice his brother to push him. Ankle-deep antics invariably, and almost instantly, progressed to a fall or a tackle and the inevitable submerged wrestling match. Yet, when I'd stage whisper, "Ducks, eleven o'clock," they'd clamber dripping and shivering to the blind in time for me to get a shot or two before the next round.

The Lagoon wasn't just a place for determined dogs and rambunctious kids to express their genetic destiny. It was, and remains, an amazing place to observe as well as participate in the lives and occasional deaths of so many species.

Eagles were a constant. They were complicit in our pursuit of ducks. They were also our competitors.

On sunny, windless days, ducks gathered offshore, en masse, teasing us. Small groups approaching the Lagoon would swing by, skimming the outer edge of our range. They'd give our dekes a dismissive glance, then spiral in to join the big flocks floating safely distant from blinds and guns.

We'd eagerly add to the babble of mallards, widgeon, and ever-present seagulls with loud but ultimately unconvincing calls of our own, but it took our winged partners to stir things up. I assume this is where the phrase about being a sitting duck originated. When the shadow of an eagle crosses a raft of ducks, there is no hesitation. The eruption of ducks seeking safety in flight is exciting. In the ensuing eagle induced quacking, whistling, panic, our spread of calm looking decoys and plaintive invitations would often be attractive enough to get a small group or two to arc in. On good days, which is to say windy ones, singles and doubles would continue to look our way for company despite dogs fetching among the decoys.

Without eagles, we'd have watched more and shot less.

The big birds were compensated for their help, too.

My dogs are fine and tenacious retrievers when we shoot well and ducks drop as intended. But Fouseks don't seem to mark longer falls as well as Labs and Chessies, so a hit bird that stays aloft another shotgun range past the decoys before crashing down requires a kayak retrieve, and a race with the eagles.

That partnership with raptors worked well for both sides. An occasional duck being carried to the top of a fir is fair compensation for their assist with sedentary flocks. We'd count the occasional eagle-seized duck against our limits, and happy to do it.

Injured or unattended dead ducks don't just attract eagles. Seagulls' frenzied response to a wounded duck is brutal. A lone eagle snatching an injured or dead duck from the water's surface is graceful, even elegant. It seems appropriate. A seagull gang is a noisy, screeching, wing flapping fight that ends with a blanket of feathers on the water's surface and a shredded duck. No one, including the unsatisfied seagulls, seems happy with the result.

Otters never approached any of our downed ducks but often added to the pleasure of the day. One morning, at the inside blind, the water's surface still as a painting, I watched an otter cruising slowly a foot below the surface. As it approached, a constant stream of tiny bubbles trailed back from its nose, a curved line of silvery, breaking bubbles, the size of 7½ shot, the only blemish on the surface. When it was abreast of me, we made eye contact. The otter didn't panic, but instead shifted into stealth mode. It maintained the same pace and heading, but the bubbles instantly stopped. It was a behavior I'd never seen, but one I'll not forget.

With ducks, eagles, shorebirds, herons, cormorants, swans, geese, otters, seals, crabs, salmon smolts, and songbirds, we were never alone.

Without my needing to say a word, my kids, grandkids, and assorted friends, from several generations, found that binoculars in a blind are as important as shotguns and get more use.

Even in a place as vibrant and full of life as the Lagoon, there are gaps in the action. Most days the sound of laughter was more frequent than gunfire. The occasional, "Dang! I thought you were watching our backs," when a duck would zip over us from behind was always a grin inducer. Jokes and stories were interrupted by, "I bet I can throw a rock farther than you." Seeing who could throw a rock closest to a floating feather, or hit the farthest decoy, were other standards. These competitions would end when a quick, whispered, "Ducks over the causeway," caused us to scramble back to the blind and still the dog.

Twenty questions was a staple in the early years. Later, when cell phones changed the world, we'd quiz each other with online trivia sites as well.

Days that started in morning darkness with donuts from the all-night grocery store just three miles from the Lagoon, lasted until afternoon light began to fade, yet rarely seemed long enough.

Good duck numbers, the confidence, or at least bravado, of teenagers, and a challenge from me started another Lagoon tradition. When one of us got within one duck of a limit, we'd switch to left-handed.

That led to more laughter, a few extra shells expended, and a lot of ducks passing unmolested as we'd wait for just the right shot.

The frequency of limits declined as priorities changed.

At the Lagoon, milestones piled up like empty shotgun shells, each a short story. Some ended with laughter, others with the death of a beautiful bird.

The emotional impact inherent in taking a life is, I think, less with birds and fish than with mammals, especially large mammals, but duck hunting can teach and expose in a way other pastimes cannot.

That may be the essential value in a place like the Lagoon. Shooting ducks was the premise, but participation was the prize.

Learning the smells, sights, and sounds of dawn on a shallow salty finger of Puget Sound matters. Recognizing birds, waterfowl or others, at distance becomes second nature, a lifetime gift.

A small flock on the horizon is "ducks" or more likely just "birds" to beach walkers, but pintails' or mallards' distinctive wing beats and silhouettes affect the posture and pulse of a hunter. A hunter comes to know cormorants and buffleheads, mergansers and herons with interest in them as individuals, not as generic birds.

A duck hunter has time. Time to recognize different duck species before shooting. Time to consider whether to shoot at the fast-closing teal or to hope the distant pair of pintails will present a chance. It doesn't seem a momentous decision, but it's a big deal to the teal.

The sharp edge of character is honed when facing life and death choices. Is the range appropriate? I'm weak on left to right shots, should I pass this opportunity? Should I look for a different target because I know my partner will also be drawn to the obvious duck?

With all this comes the sometimes-harsh acknowledgement, the guilt of failure, when the tenacity of a wounded duck can't be overcome despite dogs, shotguns, kayaks, or awkwardly wading chest deep in icy water, just a bit over wader tops.

Colt will likely retrieve fewer ducks than his predecessors; but when he's an old dog dozing in the sun, I hope flashes and fragments of days at the Lagoon will cause a little tail wag.

Finn and Avery will enjoy sun-up pastries, trivia, rock throwing, and their first shot at a decoying duck over different water, but that's okay. They got to play in the water, marvel at the iridescence of a teal's face, muddy their boots, and soak their sleeves reaching for sand dollars in the place their dad, their grandpa, and their great-grandpa first hunted waterfowl.

Next season, I hope to have another day at the Lagoon; I'll take Colt, too. We might even start at the inside blind where the pink shorebirds we've never identified hang out. When ducks approach, I'll peek over the top board, then choose my target. I'll let them circle one more time to get even closer. I'll pass the obvious duck, just because. As their feet stretch toward the water, I'll stand and watch them flare. Though I won't have my shotgun, I'm still a hunter, and this is still a hunter's place.

Road Birds

"So, how'd you do?"

The bouquet of fancy tailfeathers poking from the back of Glenn's bulging vest indicated he'd done better than me.

"Oh, Kevin," Glenn began, in his usual exuberant manner, "I had some beautiful dog work. I got birds on two solid points after long tracks, then a freebee when a rooster made the mistake of flying nearby while I was walking back. How 'bout you?"

"There are a lot of pheasants up there," I said, turning my head and tilting my chin toward the upper reaches of the hill behind me, "but there's still as many as there were this morning."

I'd rendezvoused with Glenn the previous evening after a long, day and a half drive from my coastal home. I hunt more chukars than pheasants, so I was excited to chase ringnecks. It had been a while.

We'd split up a few hours earlier because, even though I'm recently social security eligible, Glenn is several years older than me, and we cover ground at different speeds…I couldn't have kept up with him.

I did see a lot of big, flashy Montana ringnecks though.

My dog Clancy worked hard and had a number of points where roosters held long enough for me to get there if I'd been operating more efficiently, but I was hampered by a worn-out knee. That knee has since been updated with new parts. Next season, I'll get to those points.

And I will be back next season. Despite the highway miles from my home, the hunting is just too good to ignore.

I hadn't hunted Montana for several years. Had my knee been working better, I'd have kicked myself in the rear for letting that much time pass.

I met Glenn years ago when I bought my first Cesky Fousek from him. Glenn and his wife Lila are long time Montanans. He has an extensive and detailed mental map of honey holes all over the state. The stubble on the eastern edge of Montana we strode that first morning was one of them.

When we arrived, Glenn pointed up the hill. He told me there were good brush patches hidden in swales the contours hid from our parking spot. As he and his dog Addy walked toward the sun, I plodded over the first rise. As soon as I topped out, three roosters got up from the stubble between me and the brush that lined the draw below.

A good sign, I thought, as I marked where they glided into the prairie grass near the crest of the next hillside on the far side of the draw. When another, bigger bunch of pheasants cackled out of the brushy edge, I was more impressed thinking, *Dang, if only I was a little closer*. Clancy was still thirty yards from the woody brush and rose-filled dip where the stubble was replaced by native flora. I was about that far behind him when the draw erupted.

I didn't try to count, nor would it have mattered. If I picked a number based on what I saw, you'd consider me a liar or a fool. I just stared. Pheasants flushed as though from a 100-yard-wide trap house operated by a maniac. Some flew left, some right, close to the ground and high, all flying generally away.

I stood watching the most airborne pheasants I'd ever seen in one place turn from brown or brightly colored birds to little dots over a golden hillside.

Even after that mass exodus, there were still enough stragglers in the bottom and on the edges that, had I not seen the exodus, I would have still considered it a pretty darn good spot.

Over the next hill was another draw, also stiff with pheasants, and another after that.

The morning wore on while Clancy pointed. One bird after another—a surprising and frustratingly high percentage of which were roosters. I felt bad for him. He was great, doing everything right. He had earned retrieves, and I wasn't providing them. He pointed, held, then stood and watched them flush before I could get to him.

Despite my empty game bag, it was an incredible morning and, ultimately, the catalyst I needed to finally schedule the knee repair.

The next day, Glenn and I both had other mid-Montana places to be in the evening, so for our abbreviated hunt, we drove west to an intriguing block management area Glenn had only seen on a map but had been meaning to explore.

Rather than stubble and cuts, this area was mostly grass with windbreak tree lines. It didn't look as birdy as the rolling hills of the previous day, and it wasn't. Not even close. But it doesn't take roosters in triple digits to make a good day.

Glenn followed Addy toward the southern horizon while I put the sun at my back and headed off at a right angle to his track.

It turned out to be a lucky choice, as it wasn't long before I began to add illustrated pages to my internal book of memories. I was just a few minutes from the truck when Clancy got birdy.

A consistent wind carried bird scent from a distance. Clancy stood tall, head high, taking in the breeze. He knew birds were nearby yet far enough away that he was unwilling to commit. His caution worked out well for a slow-moving hunter. Each time Clancy stopped to sift the zephyrs, I'd whoa him, eliminate the gap between us, then work into the breeze in front of Clance, shotgun at port arms. I'd kick the grass in a 30-yard arc until satisfied we hadn't caught up yet, then I'd release him. He'd race ahead to where I stood, pass me by, then slow to resume his careful search; nose up in the wind weaving, not quartering.

Usually, Clancy swings much wider to the sides, but this time he confined himself to a narrow, scent-filled corridor. His right to left coverage didn't exceed 30 feet and rarely approached that.

Four times over a sizeable chunk of Montana prairie I asked Clancy to whoa. Each time we'd repeat the choreography. The last time, when I released him, he drifted by me then quickly slammed into a no nonsense, "There they are!" point. Everything about him was definite, much more emphatic than his previous, less intense, "They're out there" postures.

He was so firm in his conviction that I expected a close flush, but when the covey of huns got up, they were still more than full choke range from Clancy's classy point. Fortunately, I was a lot closer than that and was able to knock down a pair.

The second covey a little later was a condensed replay of the first. I only had to stop Clancy twice before his passionate and productive point netted me another hun.

Inspired by the dog work, pleased with the results, and aware of the time, I started back. On the way to meet Glenn at the trucks, we had the wind at our backs. Clancy was working big, out front, quartering the tall grass at a run when he abruptly turned hard left, crept a few steps back in my direction, then locked up. I walked in expecting another covey of huns but was surprised by a lone sharptail, which I managed to add to the bag.

I was feeling good. Clance was having a ball, and my vest contained two species. Four birds total, and I only had five empties in my pocket. Numbers like that move my average in an unfamiliar direction. And Clancy was enjoying showing off his nose, style, and, unlike the day before, getting to retrieve.

I was in full on "heading to the truck" mode when I saw the top of a brush patch poking out of what at first appeared to be a small draw. As I approached, I could see it was the top of a coulee that ran into a dry wash the undulating landscape had concealed. Steep terrain dictated that I approach partway down the draw. The brush and hillsides restricted my shooting to only a couple of open lanes, but it was the best option for a shot if birds were hiding in the tangle. I still had the wind at my back, but Clancy had looped around to the other side of the bushes to orient himself nose first into the wind.

Once in a while, the action seems almost scripted. I got to the spot I'd picked, then watched and listened. When Clance slowed then tensed into a point, all I could pick out through the brambles was part of the horizontal line of his back. He was well within range, maybe too close, but there was no way for me to move in for the flush. If I took even one step into the draw to roust the bird, I'd have no shot. Any other move on my part would eliminate the few shooting openings I had. With low expectations but high tension, I opted just to stand my ground. So did Clancy. It was an ancient tableau—hunter, dog, and unseen prey, all frozen, waiting.

The pheasant blinked first. He cackled when he crashed through the branches as only a big old prairie ringneck can, straight up into one of the few gaps—a riot of racket and color against blue Montana sky.

Clancy made the easy retrieve, and we ended the day, heck it was just two hours, with five birds representing three species. Pretty good for a gimpy hunter on unfamiliar ground.

Any morning where a hunter can bag three kinds of birds is pretty darn good. Even better is knowing that days like that are not unique to Montana. More than once, while we wandered clearcuts and creek bottoms in southern British Columbia, Clancy retrieved spruce, blue, and ruffed grouse on the same day. Sometimes we've even deleted one of the forest grouse from the bag on those B.C. expeditions, then filled the void with a sharptail. I live in Washington, where valley quail, chukars, and huns have often shared space in my vest.

It's not just the birds that make travelling to hunt so much fun; it's seeing new country, eating gas station tiny tacos, and having the flexibility to explore upland bird cover with minimal to no door knocking and lots of options.

Comparatively, it's not expensive either. I have friends who pay higher green fees for a single round of golf than I pay for a multi-day, non-resident bird license.

Big, huntable chunks of public land and public access to private land programs exist throughout the West. Despite no trespassing signs sprouting in appealing places and the frustration that engenders, there is opportunity for those willing to do some research.

Spreading unwieldy maps across small town café tables has morphed into squinting at cell phone screens when planning the next day's adventure, but the allure of unwalked hills and unseen arroyos spices those after dark strategy sessions with anticipation, as it always has.

As much as I like big paper maps, I have to admit, my sons have taught me that phone apps have some undeniable benefits. The precision with which a hunter in unfamiliar territory can verify property lines is a necessity. Most ranchers and farmers are the kinds of folks you wish were your neighbors, but even the nicest people get tired of armed strangers violating their space. Eliminating concern about inadvertently trespassing is a comfort, and a timesaver, for both landowners and hunters.

The pleasure and comfort of a trip is enhanced when you're free to explore while clearly aware of boundaries. Driving a rutted two track when a flock of sharptails flashes across the road to settle into a patch of wild roses above the Missouri Breaks is always fun to see. But it's better when a quick check on your phone allows you to know for sure it's okay to work your dog around to get the wind. Why, that's almost like having your own private getaway.

Whether your taste runs to the forest grouse, or sharptails of Canada, the native prairie birds and the immigrant huns and pheasants of the Great Plains, the broken, tilted landscape preferred by chukars, or cactus country quail of the Southwest, it's available. The birds, the land, and the truck stop tacos, all the ingredients for a terrific road bird feast.

Sharks and Marlin

"OK, I'm a white tablecloth, loafers, country club guy. I've never caught a fish in my life, and besides, Mexico? What are you nuts? Isn't that dangerous?"

"Web, your focus is skewed. Instead, try to feel that beautiful warm water as you wade into the sea. Imagine the slap and the splash of jumping mantas while you sip a fruity drink on the beach at sunset. And the fish? You're gonna love it."

Web, the only person in the world who calls me by my initials, was not off base about the incongruity of the prospect of him being offshore in the Sea of Cortez in a panga. Marlin fishing based on the Baja Peninsula was as far out of his experience and comfort zone, even his comprehension, as his recent trip to Scotland to play the Old Course at St. Andrews would be for me. That juxtaposition made me even more eager to convince him to give it a try.

I get a kick out of seeing things I've long enjoyed through the eyes of someone absorbing the sights, sounds, and, in this case, feeling the power and heart of a marlin, for the first time.

Seeing a clay pigeon fracture at the shot, releasing an arrow from a recurve bow to see it hit where you willed it, and being connected to a fish that really fights, are potentially life altering experiences. Whether those firsts lead to lifelong participation or are just a one off, it's a given that rookies almost universally enjoy their first time. By including the prospect of shrimp tacos, guac, a sea full of marlin, turtles, flying fish, and dolphins, then cooling off with a banana daiquiri in my pitch, I didn't see how Web could even consider declining my offer.

I was once faced with a similar situation, Steve, a good friend from my youth, and I had gone different directions after high school. Years later, a chance encounter, and the ensuing conversation, led to my first foray for Mexican marlin. I was nervous about the prospect of seasickness and dreaded Montezuma's revenge, but Steve, a veteran of multiple trips, calmed me down and convinced me to go. I caught my first marlin that trip. It remains the smallest I've seen. But the impact that fish had on me was huge. Though small for its kind, it was still, by a bunch, the biggest fish I'd ever encountered. It jumped and, as this incredible, stunning animal hung suspended over the water, a whale surfaced and spouted just beyond.

I was as hooked as that fish.

I haven't been back every year since that first time, but I haven't missed many years either.

My first return trip was almost exactly twelve months later.

Pat and Keith joined Steve and me. Neither had fished much, and never sub-tropical salt water, and neither had been to Baja. The four of us hired a cruiser the first day so we could all fish together. Steve and I deferred to the new guys. They would be first up. After the various drawing of straws, the order was set. Pat was first, Keith, Steve, then me.

We had barely left the dock when noise and dark smoke emanating from inappropriate places in our boat led to a shut down. As we drifted, silently, without power, engulfed in the noxious brown cloud that enveloped our disabled craft, there was much discussion over the radio in loud and frequently strident Spanish. We didn't understand the words, but the frustration in those voices was clear. By the time we were towed back to the dock and another boat was lined up, a precious part into our fishing day had melted away.

In those early years, I had not yet reached the age, the level of enlightenment, or had sufficient marlin in my background, that would allow me to enjoy watching my companions fight a fish with as much pleasure as if I were on the rod myself. I really wanted to catch a fish. I couldn't even make a credible attempt of pretending. I was also keenly aware that we had split the cost of the boat and the bait equally. By the time we finally got squared away with a working vessel and headed out I was bummed, convinced my prospects of tangling with a billfish that day had evaporated, along with my quarter of the cost.

Pat caught a rambunctious marlin soon after we started trolling. Within an hour of releasing that first fish, Keith was tied into his first striped marlin. Keith's fish was a jumper. Jumpers wear out quicker than fish that battle from below. Despite our late start, I was beginning to see a glimmer of hope.

The morning's fast start was a tease. As the hours and the engine droned on, it began to feel as though that glimmer, like a shiny, shimmery vision of water on a desert highway, was a mirage. We had already passed the time that would usually signal a return to shore when, to my surprise, the skipper said we'd keep going. Despite our smokey start, he wanted us to get a whole day of fishing. My prospects had suddenly increased from seemingly non-existent to merely unlikely. Even with the extra time, considering the complete lack of any action for hours, I was resigned to being a bystander. Steve, even though he was on deck, metaphorically and literally, was checking his watch frequently, too.

When a marlin suddenly appeared in our wake among the trolled baits and teasers, the deck hand threw a live bait and was instantly tight to the third fish of the day. Steve, the old hand of our crew, wrestled his fish well and, for a triple digit fish, quickly. With a photo and an immediate "adios" to the fish, I expected we were done.

It was now hours past time to head back but still a few minutes short of the total a normal start time would have provided. I could see the skipper and the deck hand calculating. To their credit, and my gratitude, they set up to troll though they, and I, were aware it was the longest of longshots.

I knew we'd pick up the gear in minutes, but that turned out to be enough. Tail fins of two marlin slashed the calm water close by to starboard. Live bait worked again. As unlikely as it seemed, there I stood at the back of the deck, with the butt of the rod tucked into a fighting belt, feeling the violent, pulsing weight and strength of the fish while watching the line on the spool spin away as the striper made its first long run. When it finally stopped taking line, this fish fought deep and hard. By the time I got it to the boat, the sun was almost touching the mountain tops to the west.

Four hookups, with four marlin brought to the boat and released. The classy captain and mate making sure we got our full measure, then an improbable last-minute hook up and prolonged fight that extended our time on the water even further. A terrific day after a suspect start.

The skipper and hand hustled to put up the tackle. They tossed the remaining bait overboard, got the marlin flags flying on the outriggers, then slammed the throttle to the stops and triumphantly, and eagerly, pointed the bow toward shore.

The lowering sun may have caused some glare on the surface, probably a contributing factor to what happened next. We were going as fast as that old wooden cruiser would go when we crashed into the whale shark.

Seeing the gigantic fish rolling in our wake confirmed that we'd hit a shark and not a submarine, but it was a dramatic jolt. The instant question: were we seaworthy?

I am not good at judging distance over water, especially in what was becoming an even lower light situation. The exact number of miles didn't matter. A long way from shore, and too far to swim, was a good enough estimate.

While we had been enjoying our extended fishing day, none of us noticed the diminishing radio chatter and eventual dead air, or the lack of silhouettes of other fishing boats on the horizon. Now, that silence and solitude seemed foreboding.

The boat was damaged, but, at least as of the initial triage, remained dry inside. The engine fired but the prop or the shaft was bent so badly, the skipper was forced to run at barely above an idle. Even a slight increase in RPMs rattled the already shaky craft and made noises that shouted at him to slow down.

Though banged up and a couple of us slightly bloodied from getting knocked off our seats on impact, we were in better shape than the boat. Once we determined we weren't going to spend any time treading mile deep water brimming with big, toothy fish, we enjoyed a jovial, walking speed, moonlight cruise back to the dock.

That was my first encounter with a whale shark. With all the hubbub, I didn't even get a good look at it. Years later, my daughter Megan and I had a serendipitous encounter with whale sharks where we got up close and personal.

Growing up, Megan had caught trout and a salmon or two, but since she'd graduated from college and moved to San Diego, we hadn't fished together for some time. She's always ready to try something new, so no convincing was required. When I called, I said, "You want to meet me in Mexico to—"

"Yup," she said. "When?"

We had a good time. In addition to catching school size dorado and powerful, relentless rooster fish, we snorkeled with sea-lions, ate dorado sashimi from fish we caught, and kayaked a beautiful bay.

With nothing scheduled for our last day, except late flights north, we looked through the offerings of a kiosk-based tour operator. When we asked to set up a "swim with whale sharks" excursion, his response was a firm, "No." It was May, an unlikely time to find sharks. After some haggling and our repeated assurance that there would be no hard feelings if we were sharkless, he relented. We watched frigatebirds floating above the marina while he made multiple calls to track down a crew. When our skiff finally rounded the breakwater, it was just Meg, me, the skipper, and Sophia, an enthusiastic young naturalist.

They went through the motions appropriately, but our crew was truly surprised when we found a group of three sharks basking on the surface in the warm late morning sun. Rather than passing through, this trio was content to hang out. The water was clear and warm. We swam with them for hours, taking an occasional break for a drink of water and a breather, but we never tired due to the sharks not wanting to leave. We floated more than swam with them. Though docile, Sophia admonished us to stay near their heads. An inadvertent swipe of a tail having the potential to be an unforgettable slap if we got too close.

We did get close—really close. Being nudged aside by the world's biggest fish is thrilling. Massive schools of sardines would periodically envelope the sharks in a shimmering, silvery cloud, then instantly part, like opening a curtain, to reveal the spotted giants, only to return moments later. When they opened their wide mouths to take in gulps of plankton rich water, we could see remoras hanging from their palates.

Suspended in the warm, shallow water of that blue green bay in the company of fish the size of an airstream and uncountable baitfish is a Mexican moment neither of us will forget.

Kind of like Dave the golfer, when I asked Trish and Greg to join my wife Laurie and me, I expected to hear a "That sounds great…but no thanks" sort of response. They are frequent and adventurous travelers. They've been all over the world, often involving long distance tandem bike riding and wine. I'd never known either to show any interest in fishing. Since I knew they'd be fun companions, I asked anyway.

They didn't hesitate. They were instantly onboard. That first trip, Greg and I got skunked, but the ladies both caught wahoo. That evening, toasting our great day, reliving being surrounded by dolphins, and feasting on wahoo fillets, I could tell by the grins and storytelling that Baja had worked her magic on our friends. On a subsequent trip, everyone caught marlin. Laurie and Trish each had a two billfish day, and Greg got to compare and contrast the strength and style of a marlin with the determined brawling of a rooster fish on consecutive days. When he released his rooster over the gunwale, he gave me a tired smile, shook his head, then said, "I don't think I would ever get a really big rooster to the boat."

I don't know if I would either, but oh man, I sure would like to try.

"So, what do you say, Web? Is June good for you, or would July be better?"

There was a long silence on the line. I thought maybe we'd lost our phone connection. Finally, "Alright, KK, you got me. I'm in," he said. "Let's do this Mexico thing."

Web is an East Coast guy, and I'm in the Pacific Northwest. When we met at the airport in Mexico, it was apparent that he was game, but still a little apprehensive.

The hour and a half drive north in our rental car did little to reassure him. The severe landscape of cactus, sand, and mountains with skinny cows and goats, both alongside and crossing the road, were all new to him, and apparently not comforting.

At the hotel, everything was in good order in our room. There was a bar and pool on site, with the long, wide, sandy, and mostly empty beach a few steps below. No livestock in sight. He was back in his element and visibly relaxed.

That evening, we did indeed have shrimp tacos, then hoisted an adult beverage or two while watching mantas jump just offshore, hearing their distinctive reentry plop a fraction of a second after they disappeared. My credibility was intact, possibly enhanced.

The next day, though our timing was good, as was our skipper, we saw just one marlin. It jumped a couple of times astern but never approached, then moved on. Dolphins, turtles, flying fish, and frigatebirds kept us entertained, so it was a pleasant, but fish free day.

Web was fine, it had been a good day, but as we walked from the boat to the hotel, I was concerned. In other introductions I'd come to value the benefit of quick reinforcement. Get a guy on a fish, and he may well become a fisherman; take him on a boat ride, no matter how pleasant, the odds go down. Fun but lacking that addictive adrenaline spike.

That first day was, well, it wasn't "rough" water, but it was bouncy. Enough so that when moving around the panga, it was necessary to hold on.

The second, and our final day, was a bit bouncier. Not at all scary, but in a small boat it can be tiring, might even qualify as an ab workout. Worse though, it's harder to spot a marlin tail poking out of the water when it's camouflaged in waves.

Like the previous day, it was "nice," but unease kept me from enjoying the abundance of sea life as much as I normally do. Like that day decades ago, I felt opportunity slipping away.

I have finally reached the stage of maturity, enlightenment, whatever it might be called, where, while I still really want to catch a fish, I would trade my next two for Web to catch one. I viscerally needed Web to fight a marlin. A fish for him, and I'd consider it mission accomplished.

Again, the end of our time on the water was staring us in the face. There had been no marlin action all day. Nada.

Last minute marlin are the best. A fin gouged the face of a wave just yards away. Any further and we'd never have noticed. A cast, a moment of uncertainty, then, "YES!" a marlin ripping line.

Web sat in the fighting chair, beautifully, wonderfully, rattled and wildly out of his element. He hunched over so far, his face nearly touched the reel. He cranked the reel as fast as he could, while the marlin was taking line the other way.

Five minutes in, he finally understood to stop reeling when losing line. He twisted to look at me, eyes wide, and said, "KK, take the rod for a while."

"Not a chance buddy, all you."

He rallied from there. With a little coaching, he was soon upright in his seat and getting in synch with that rocking rhythm of bending the rod up then reeling down. It was not a big fish by striped marlin standards, but not small either—a legit standard bearer of his kind nobly doing what marlin do.

The fish fought hard. It didn't jump after an initial display. Web made progress, would start believing he'd won, then a moment later he'd just breathe deeply and hang on with both hands as the marlin reclaimed all the line he had gained and a little more.

The sound of the motor and the splash of the waves was intermittently overshadowed by Web blurting various one- and two-word obscenities, a reversion to the golfer in him I suspect.

Eventually when Web gained line, the duration of the subsequent runs decreased. As the curtain rose on the third act, the action moved to the surface. Web gained confidence along with line.

With the fish finally alongside, the skipper grabbed the bill, instantly eliminating the weight on the line. Web slumped, briefly, shook his arms and shoulders, then rallied for the obligatory photo before sliding his first ever marlin back into the clear blue Sea of Cortez.

That was it. Minutes later, the marlin flag was flying, and we were, too. Heading for the beach. Web recovered quickly. He was jacked! He high fived, then fist bumped me, massaged his forearms, fist bumped again, then once more, just because. His excitement showed in his face and in every move and comment he made.

I shared a philosophical message where I told him savor this moment. He was different now, forever connected to the Sea of Cortez, not just a visitor, but part of it.

The engine noise at go home speed and bouncing on the waves made hearing each other a little tough, but even with the background noise he made a point to lean in for his next, just between us, comment. I expected a follow up, an acknowledgement of my impressively deep and pithy reference.

"KK," he said, "I think toward the end of the fight, the skipper called me Senorita."

Talisman

"It's weird, Megan, that your dad has dead animals all over the place. Doesn't it creep you out?"

Remembering the power of peers, I was pleased and a little surprised that Megan, my then thirteen-year-old daughter, didn't seem particularly bothered by her friend's assessment of the hairy and antlered accents to our home décor. She answered, "I think they're pretty."

Her friend's comment, snarky and judgmental as it was, is a typical, though less nuanced, version of a pervasive attitude about the things some urban folks find uncomfortable in the homes, and the minds, of hunters.

By "urban," I don't mean one who lives in a city. I live in an incorporated town with neighbors all around. Being pseudo-urban, or at least suburban, myself, as are most of my friends, I don't mean it to be derogatory either. It's simply a convenient catch-all term to denote a cultural perspective that discounts or disdains the archaic notion that it's okay to kill some of what we eat, and to enjoy that pursuit. Even less acceptable is the taxidermy that occasionally follows. Paradoxically, antlers are in vogue with many of these same sophisticates who recognize and appreciate their curvaceous and pointy appeal. Antlers or horns must not, however, in polite company, be attached to a mounted head or bleached skull, and are sometimes (shudder) painted.

I'm resistant—though not entirely immune—to contrary opinions, so I have pondered whether they have a point. Is there something slightly off, something that a normal, twenty-first century American could reasonably consider weird, about displaying mounted heads on my walls, and by extension, me? I guess the answer depends on what constitutes "normal" and "reasonably." Eccentric seems fair, I guess, maybe even quirky in some contexts, but weird, creepy, even gross? I don't think so.

I'm no anthropologist, but experience, fortified by paying attention, has shown me that collecting and displaying physical reminders of memorable events and travels is a common human trait.

It isn't just about reminiscence though; there's an aspect of aspiration as well. In Don Thomas's terrific book, *Longbows in the Far North*, he discusses a puzzle regarding the cave paintings of Lascaux. Scenes depicted on the walls of those French caverns, though thousands of years old, still ignite academic debate over whether the artist's intent was to create, by magic, a desired outcome, or to memorialize the past.

Maybe it's both. Antlers on my wall trigger treasured memories, but they also remind, no, they goad me, to plan my next trip into the backcountry.

The rack of a Shiras moose hangs in my kitchen. Some guests in my home have been confused and bothered by that. First because, like my daughter's unfiltered friend, they have been persuaded by the "hunting is murder" crowd but also because it is so unexpected. It's like finding a shrunken head next to the salad fork on your table in a fancy restaurant, or being greeted at Starbucks by a barista holding a tiger on a leash. The incongruity confounds.

Others are befuddled that someone as nice and seemingly normal as my wife tolerates such anachronistic foolishness.

I'm grateful that I married wisely.

While antlers and head mounts are novelties to many, maybe "triggers" to some visitors to our home, my choice to use the wall space my wife allocated to me to display things that fire up memories and spark desires is not unique.

A friend's home features long, wooden skis crossed on the river rock façade above the fireplace to remind them, and visitors alike, of the beauty and history of snow, speed, and the promise of next winter.

Another friend exhibits grass baskets hand woven in the 1800s by the mothers of her grandma's playmates. They were old when given to her mom nearly one hundred years ago. When I asked about them, years slid from her cloudy eyes as she talked about using similar baskets while picking berries with her Makah neighbors.

Her mental images, though faded, were intact, but as she held and turned the baskets, her old fingers lightly tracing the intricacy of the weave, the corporeal truth of those baskets enhanced her reminiscing as well as my pleasure in her storytelling.

Ceramic or leather elephants adorn the living rooms of some who have travelled to Thailand or Laos. Masks from African trips glare from places of prominence, and it's a rare home or office that doesn't include photographs of people, places, or events that have earned a spot in the history of the curator of each individual gallery…or of places and adventures conceived, gestating, but yet, unborn.

Don, a Montana friend, has prioritized better than most of us. He and his wife have hunted, fished, and photographed all over the world. His combination of effort and skill have left him with more antlers, horns, prime hides, and artifacts than he has room to display but, in his home, a disproportionate amount of wall space bristles with the spiky hair and curved tusks of pigs from several continents.

I asked about them once. He didn't try to explain or convince me of their porcine allure, he just said, "I like pigs."

Having never hunted pigs, I don't yet share his passion for pork on the hoof. I think I get it though.

The import and impact of memories and mementos are different for each of us. It's hard to understand the enchantment of another's totems.

I'm not talking about souvenirs.

The disparity is not only difficult to describe, it isn't even consistent. That ceramic elephant on the bookshelf of someone who left the bustle of Bangkok for a multi-day elephant encounter means something quite different than that same tchotchke picked up at a crowded zoo concession after a ten-minute howdah ride.

On vacation with my parents when I was a boy, with five whole dollars I was given to spend as I chose, I bought a beautiful painting. In retrospect, it was a tin serving platter sporting a print of a whitetail buck. Though it still hangs at our cabin, I have no recollection of where we were when I got it. It's a souvenir. It's an appropriate cabin decoration that I still like, but devoid of meaning.

My first inkling of the importance, the psychic impact, of tangible connections to the past, or hoped for futures, was the result of an impulse.

The summer after my freshman year in college, my dog died. We'd been a team for a long time, from my first days as a cub scout.

I'd scored a job that summer working swing shift at a lumber mill. I arrived home one night at my usual time, a bit after midnight, to find Nikki lying dead in the yard near where I parked, as though waiting for me one last time. With her head on my lap, despite her stiffening neck, we drove to what was a special place for the two of us where, on that moonless August night, I scratched out her grave. Before lowering her, with no forethought or plan, I unbuckled her collar.

That essentially unconscious choice would someday matter more than my nineteen-year-old self that night could have imagined.

When we were twenty somethings, my buddy Stu and I stopped to visit an old guy living in an out of the way corner of the guiding area in British Columbia Stu had recently purchased. Bill, the definition of a hermit, was pleased with the prospect of guests. He invited us in. He pushed a kettle to a hotter part of his woodstove. While the water warmed, he skittered around the cabin gathering the requirements for this impromptu tea party. Using his forearm, he shoved a bunch of magazines, a stirrup, and two cats off the table, then poured us each a cup of tea. As we drank his tea and ate from a tin of cookies, Bill shared stories of moose, bears, mountain goats, and mishaps. Three cups of tea and many tales in, Bill offered to show us his museum.

He led us out back through shin high, late May grass to a tired, bent over shack covering a footprint no bigger than the bed of a pickup. He flashed a snaggly grin over his shoulder, and his old eyes glistened with anticipation as he lifted the slightly mossy 2x4 crossbar from its bracket to allow the doors of his exhibit to screech open.

It wasn't what I expected. Given what I'd seen in his home, I would have been surprised had it been nicely laid out, but I did think there might be a shelf or two; certainly something a bit more organized than the random junk pile it appeared to be.

The first curio he sorted out from this hoarder's dream was a five-foot-long gnarled branch with a bend near the top.

"I found this shillelagh up on Redband Mountain near fifty years ago, been in my collection ever since." Stu and I made what we hoped were approving noises.

He was clearly fond of that stick, but there was more, so much more. After sharing several other mementos, including a smaller but very similar stick, for smaller fights no doubt, he extracted from the jumble his favorite. It was a caved in, rusted, three-pound, campfire-charred coffee can with a bailing wire handle.

His already creaky voice faltered with emotion as he told us, "My old horse Dan," Bill paused, sucked in a shaky breath, then continued, "he stepped on this up Grizzly Creek way…it's a nice keepsake." The last part barely a whisper.

Despite my spontaneous rescue of Nikki's collar a few years prior, I was callow and still a bit too sophisticated to appreciate Bill and his sentiment.

Visceral understanding of the weight of personal talismans takes time.

Memories of Bill's sticks and cockeyed coffee can linger though, not because of their beauty, nor because of how I perceived their oddness, though I admit, at the time, that was what struck me. No, I remember Bill's Museum because of its obvious importance to him.

The day after our visit with Bill, I shot a bear. He was a mature boar with a large skull and the impossibly thick and deep black hide that interior British Columbia bears wear in the spring. That bear was the realization of a long-held ambition. It wasn't my first bear, but it was my rug.

I love bears. Since I was kid, black bears have had a hold on me. Hearing or saying, "There's a bear!" generates a jolt I hope I never get over.

The first bear I ever stalked and killed was modest sized with a thin coat. I'd prowled many huckleberry fields before I finally spotted this bear a long way off. I was able to sneak into range and made a good shot. That little bear was a rite of passage for me. I had done the things a hunter does: I got a bear.

That berry-fed bear was great on the grill, but his pelt was not the rug I craved.

I don't recall the process, but a friend showed me how to do a shoddy and ultimately short-term tanning job. Despite the small size and a slight odor, I was glad to have it. That patch of black fur, with manila folder colored skin showing through the hairless parts, hung on various hooks and nails in my homes for years. It was both a reminder of the day, and a harbinger of the rug in my future. Eventually the hide dissolved. The claws were the only part I could salvage.

Those curved black claws went into a cigar box with Nikki's collar.

That collar and those claws remained in that box, until I needed them.

The dogs I've lived with since were loved more completely and mourned more profoundly than if I'd not had my eight-year-old heart captured by Nikki's warm breath and puppy whiskers in my ear, then first experienced true grief at her loss.

The imperfect man I am is better than any alternative version of myself who never knew bears. Bears at any distance boost adrenaline, but the pucker inducing sounds, smells, and sights of black and grizzly bears up close and upset, impart lessons and confirm or expose facets of oneself that are worthwhile to know.

So, in a time of desperate need, when I retrieved that collar and those claws, they gave me comfort.

This quintessential human trait of imbuing things, charms, with power, meaning, or just sentiment, transcends time and cultures. Ancient Egyptians packed for the afterlife as though they were the early twentieth century Rockefellers preparing for a transatlantic cruise. Ishi, the last Yana Indian, per his wishes, was cremated with his bow, five arrows, a basket of acorn meal, and dried venison. Things he might need in unfamiliar territory.

During some rough days, I thought about an old hermit's squashed coffee can. I remembered Ishi outfitting for the happy hunting ground. Memories and preparation.

As I stood looking down, I imagined dogs he would never love, dogs who wouldn't share his sleeping bag on a cold night. I felt regret for the excitement, the awe, at spotting a bear, an atavistic stirring he wouldn't know. Then I nestled those black bear claws and Nikki's collar next to the tiny, impossibly cold hands of the doll-like body of my infant son. I slowly closed the lid, incensed and broken at how perverse, how outrageous, that the only thing I'd ever buy for him was an obscenely small white coffin.

With no intellectual justification or abiding faith, but no recourse, my wife and I sent our baby boy Sam, like Ishi and the Pharos, into the unknown, the unknowable, with the fervent hope that dogs and bears were waiting.

Make Mine an Old Fashioned

"You gotta be kiddin' me," I said out loud, even though I was alone in my office. I had just verified online that, for the second straight year, I did not draw a non-resident buck tag in Montana. The previous year, when I was passed over, though it wasn't exactly expected, it wasn't a surprise. Increasing demand had hammered draw odds, and I didn't have a preference point. This year I thought I was in. Alas, skunked again.

So, no buck tag for me, but a darn good consolation prize. Riley and Jake, my sons, have been applying along with me for a number of years. With three of us submitting individual applications, someone, so far, always pulls a permit. With at least one of us seeking antlers and meat, the others are available to spot, kibbitz, celebrate, and haul. In the interest of full disclosure, it's been some time since I've done much hauling. The guys get the bucks to the truck while I walk alongside taking an occasional photo, while offering unnecessary and unheeded advice.

Our bird dogs join us on these Montana trips. We humans hunt deer in the mornings and late afternoons, but mid-day, and all day after the deer tags are filled, we gang up on the sharptails and occasional huns which inhabit the same generally frosty and always sage-scented range as the mule deer.

The year before, in response to going tagless, I'd hatched a plan to hunt Big Sky deer despite my lack of luck in the lottery. I was going with the guys anyway, and there was an empty shelf in my freezer. I'd simply buy a whitetail doe tag. No luck required. They're over the counter.

There were a couple of bumps I'd need to smooth out. Nothing that couldn't be overcome, but adjustments would need to be made.

We knew the country we hunted. If one of us referred to Frozen Badger, The Corner, The Tire, Volley Valley, On Top, or, of course, The Honey Hole, we all understood the reference. We'd left boot tracks, and gut piles, in those spots. That comfortable familiarity had led to a bunch of notched tags, and a confidence that had seeped into our collective and individual psyches. The glitch was, we'd never seen a whitetail in any of those places. Though whitetail adjacent, the public badlands and prairie we roamed were mule deer country. The majority of whitetails were on private ground. We'd have to hunt for a spot before hunting for deer. It's hard to do that well from two states away.

I got lucky overcoming that dilemma. We wouldn't have to spend a day or two getting oriented after all. It turned out I knew a guy who knew a guy. With one email and a couple of phone calls, I was able to secure permission for the three of us to hunt a chunk of mixed pines, aspen, and farmland. It was entirely different terrain and vegetation than we were used to. Different vistas, smells, and different deer, an enticing change of pace. It was big, too. We had room enough to meander a bit and the property boundaries were clear, so no worry about accidental trespassing.

Along with being allowed access, whitetails were purported to be wildly abundant on the ranch. Even better, we'd have my place to ourselves. Sounded perfect.

Neither Jake nor Ri, both lucky deer-combo tag owners, had ever taken a whitetail buck. They were looking forward to the prospect of different shaped antlers. A whitetail doe for me would be, I was assured, the proverbial piece of cake.

After finding a place to hunt, that "no sweat" ease of getting a doe I'd been promised was the other fly in this new and pleasing ointment we were concocting.

I wanted venison for my table, but I didn't want to "harvest" a deer. I wanted to go deer hunting. To make this a true pursuit rather than a sure thing, I needed to stuff extra weight into this doe tag saddle.

The admonition to "be careful what you wish for" should have crossed my mind about then.

It didn't take long to figure out that the answer to how I would handicap this hunt was standing patient and ready in my safe.

In 1948, my great Uncle Joe, a man much more at home, and more stable, on a barstool than in deer country, won a rifle on a tavern punchboard. Joe had no use for a firearm. My dad, who had recently returned from a multi-year, all-inclusive cruise in the South Pacific, along with thousands of other guys his age, was nurturing a developing interest in hunting, but didn't own a rifle.

A deal was struck, and my dad became the owner of a Savage Stevens model 325C bolt action 30-30, with open sights and a 3-shot detachable magazine.

That rifle was the first firearm I ever saw or touched.

I was a little kid when my dad showed me how the bolt worked to slide a cartridge into the chamber. Then he described how to align the bead of the front sight into the tiny slit in the rear sight. I had never even shot a BB gun at that stage of my life, but Dad impressed on me the man-sized responsibility of knowing there was a rifle in our home. He asked me to promise never to touch it unless he was with me.

I never did, until I was a hunter myself.

Even before that talk, I knew the 30-30 was in the corner of my parents' closet, but that day was my official introduction. When I finally actually fired a rifle, it was also a bolt action with open sights. A Remington Nylon 12. A tube fed .22 Dad got at Nates Hardware. It had a futuristic brown nylon stock with a classy white diamond inlaid on the side, just ahead of the bolt handle. Twenty-one years later, my buddy Curley broke that .22 on the head of a coyote he'd mortally wounded with the last long rifle cartridge he had in his pocket. Prior to meeting its noble end as a coyote club, that .22 accounted for a pile of grouse, a handful of rabbits, tin cans, dump rats, and, during my hound dog days, coons. The old Savage/Stevens 30-30 passed most of those years like a hamster in a cage, appreciated, but rarely taken out.

While I was growing up, Dad worked six days a week. During my first four years as a licensed hunter, on the three deer season Sundays the state of Washington granted us each year, we shared the rifle. To avoid confusion, Dad and I worked out a detailed plan to deal with a multiple buck situation. I'd shoot first. For planning purposes, we assumed I'd make a quick and perfect shot, then I'd swiftly pass the rifle to Dad who would then drop the largest of the remaining bucks. Our plan was simple, but it seemed to cover all the necessary elements. We thought it was solid. There were not many ways for it to go wrong. We never tested the efficiency of the plan though, because during those years we never saw a buck, not even a spike. I think Dad enjoyed hunting without the bother of carrying a rifle.

When, in the '70s, the Seahawks came to a nearby town. My dad's Sundays became more about NFL football than hunting.

By then, I'd moved on to what I considered a much cooler rifle. It was also a number of years old, but it had a leather military sling, and I added a brand new 4-power Redfield Widefield scope. With that rifle, a driver's license, and like-minded buddies, I started hunting Saturdays, too.

From the day it left the factory, until now, the rifle that had so intrigued me as a boy accounted for two blacktail deer, both before I was old enough to remember, one before I was born. Other than that handful of double duty Sundays, it languished in Dad's closet. Eventually it migrated to my closet, then, when I became a dad, to my safe.

In the years since, Dad died, and I've been lucky enough to roam a lot of wild, pretty, and game rich places, with rifles, shotguns, and bows. For decades, that 30-30 remained quiet, stoic, standing at attention against the back wall of my safe. Waiting.

That old rifle, with its round nose bullets, and diabolical open sights, was just the right seasoning to spice up my quest for a whitetail doe.

This all began to make perfect sense to me. The provenance of the rifle emerged from Uncle Joe's fondness for whiskey. A 19th century cocktail, the Old Fashioned, included more ingredients than Joe required in his glass, but the bulk of both the cocktail and Joe's more…basic tastes, was the same brown beverage. The result, an uncomplicated, reliable, and somewhat dated classic that would get the job done. Just like my rifle. This would be an Old Fashioned hunt.

If things worked out as I hoped, when I squeezed the trigger on a fat doe a few months hence, it would end a long dry spell. Though both my dad and I packed that gun into the early 1970s, it had not been fired with lethal intent since 1955.

Despite the intervening decades, I intended this to be an authentic throwback. That meant no changes from when my twelve-year-old hands first cradled the slick, uncheckered grip as I wandered tall timber and soggy second growth in my red and black plaid wool jacket, day-dreaming about my first deer.

"Wandering" was how we hunted when I was a kid. I still tend to stay on the move. Creeping through the woods and edges of clearcuts and meadows has always been my preference, even though I know an ambush is more likely to produce venison. That extra wrinkle was an integral part of the deal I made with myself. If I was to fill my freezer, it would be by still hunting or spot and stalk, no taking a stand.

Ultimately, I did acquiesce to one alteration. I added a slip-on butt pad, to account for the several inches of height I had on my dad. That was it though. No sling, no pointy, ballistically superior, hand loaded bullets, and definitely no scope.

Deer hunting with a 30-30 is not some Herculean accomplishment. It's no more surprising than catching panfish with worms. Though it's fallen out of favor in the past few decades, I suspect more deer have hung on camp meat poles with 30-30 holes in their chest than any other round. The round and the rifle are both perfectly suited for deer hunting. I was the variable.

When I conceived the idea of this Old Fashioned hunt, it was as an homage to my dad, a tip of the hat to my own initiation into the lifetime of hunting, and a connection across the years through that modest little rifle. I thought it would be fun.

The best laid plans…

In my mental preamble for this 30-30 deer hunt, I'd assumed that the combination of reading glasses and the weirdly confounding sights might slightly raise the degree of difficulty. That was the point.

It turned out that I had wildly underestimated the enhanced challenge those old factory iron sights and my…experienced eyes brought to this project.

It was a revelation how much more gracefully the rifle had aged than had my betraying eyes.

When shooting bows or shotguns, no optical aid or precise aiming are required. I look where I want to hit, then make a slight movement with my hand. It works great. Typically, with a target 15 to 40 yards away, when I pull the trigger or drop the string, my brain, with a lifetime of practice, does the geometry. The arrow or the shot pattern hits generally, though sometimes a fraction less precisely than I'd like, where I intend.

The first time I shot the Savage in preparation of this quest, I found that with the rear sight, the front sight, and the target all different distances from my eye, an array of unforeseen and interesting complications arose.

Without glasses, I was able to see the target clearly, but the sights were an indecipherable mess. With my night-time reading glasses, the strong ones, the rear sight was sharp but the front sight, just a memory, the target, a blur. The weak reading glasses I use when watching TV generated results similar to my unaided eyes. I even tried weak and strong readers layered on my nose, an awkward and impractical pseudo bifocal. That, too, was no help.

Through a combination of trial and error, muscle memory, a dab of white paint on the front bead, and wishing really hard, I found that without glasses, I could produce groups that were sufficient for ethical hunting, as long as I followed my own, newly created rules. I needed good light, a solid rest, and an unaware doe within sixty steps of my muzzle. Closer would be better.

As I shot occasionally throughout the summer, my earlier concern that my doe hunt would lack suspense or uncertainty was erased. Taking a spooky whitetail under these circumstances would provide all the opportunity to fail that I needed.

When we arrived in Montana, we found the access we'd lined up was as advertised. The property was a nice blend of native grasses, trees, and ag. The only difference from what we expected was the near total lack of deer.

Heavy snow and plummeting temperatures had pushed all but the most stubborn or stupid deer to lower elevations.

Jake did earn his first whitetail buck. During a blizzard, on the first day, when the snow wasn't yet two feet deep, just at dusk. It was the only buck any of us saw that year.

We hunted hard, but the weather was relentless. Constant, freezing winds worked in concert with the ever-deeper snow to cover our tracks, tire or boot, in minutes.

We headed out each morning, more resigned than optimistic, willing to endure merciless pounding by the elements. Dawn to dusk abuse combined with a dearth of deer dampened our enthusiasm. Despite attitude buoying short windows of clear skies, when our week ran out, we were ready, maybe even a little eager, to head home.

The following spring, when I came up empty on a buck tag again, I was surprised and more than slightly peeved. I had a dang preference point; it should have been a gimmee. After minor venting about the doggone rigged system, the unfairness of it all, followed by my eventual realization that I did not, in fact, have a preference point, having missed a step in the application process, my initial frustration melted away. I forgave the drawing gods and was excited to give both me and that old rifle another chance.

I've heard that there is an innate mental mechanism that erases, or at least, alters a mother's memory of the discomfort of labor; otherwise, no one would have a younger sibling. Something like that must work in the minds of hunters. Recollections of fun, perfect stalks and shots remain while thoughts of chaining up tires, frozen fingers, howling winds, and frostbite fade.

This time the November weather in Montana was perfect, and the deer were where they were supposed to be.

Scott, a buddy of Jake and Ri, added one man and a second vehicle to this trip. With two trucks, Jake and I were free to hunt grouse in the morning while the other two, with their buck tags, returned to our old haunts looking for mule deer. Around lunch time I'd head for whitetail country while the other three, and the dogs, hunted birds.

Each afternoon I saw and stalked deer. Every blown effort evolved into another attempt. The worry I'd somehow re-kindled about this being too easy evaporated. These deer were cagey. I'd belly crawl over the last hump between me and small groups of deer to find them staring at me from 80 yards out. Easy with a scoped rifle, or for a hunter with youthful eyes, but as unreachable as the moon for me.

I had a sure thing one afternoon. Creeping along above a creek bottom, I flushed a doe from the thick growth near the stream. She bolted into an abandoned corral. With a tumbled down shed on one side, an impossible tangle of boards and brush blocking her other exit, I stood between her and escape—she was trapped, twenty yards away. We stared at each other, I even lined up on her, counting coup, then stepped back, waved her on her way, and watched her, flashing white and brown, until she was out of sight.

Ri and Scott had found and tagged their mule deer bucks. We'd all enjoyed some fine dog work and sharptail shooting, and I had been having fun sneaking around the whitetails, but the week was winding down. I was beginning to wonder what kind of a hunter can't fill a doe tag, with a rifle, in a deer rich environment.

On my last afternoon, from a half a mile away, I spotted several deer in a small patch of green that jutted off a much larger winter wheat field, like a thumb-shaped bay off a green, grassy ocean. It was narrow enough that if I could make the edge, I'd be in range. At this distance, I couldn't be sure they weren't bucks, but I thought it likely there'd be at least one bald deer in the bunch.

It was an interesting stalk. Using terrain, abandoned farm equipment, and vegetation as cover, I hustled to close the gap. If they remained where I'd last seen them, when I emerged from the steep but short draw ahead of me, I'd be on the edge of the field, and they'd be in shooting distance at my two o'clock.

I crept so quietly I silently congratulated myself. The wind, though not directly in my face, blew at an angle that was sufficient to negate their absurdly keen noses. I crept the final few feet to where I could make the shot, slowly slid my rifle over the last hummock, then looked to my right, into an empty field.

A small sound to my left drew my glance. A doe stared at me, within recurve range. An easy shot with a rifle. But when I made the rookie tactical error of direct eye contact, she instantly took two steps over the edge and was gone. She didn't spook though. The rest of the deer I'd seen were still there but at my ten o'clock rather than on the other side of the draw where I'd expected them. There were four, all does. Completely unaware, thirty steps away.

On a ranch big enough that the ground is measured in miles rather than acres, there were two horses, just two, on the whole ranch. Both of those horses grazed peacefully, with the deer, my deer, directly between me and the horses.

When I tried to reposition for a safe shot, the first doe who had quietly stepped away initially, exploded from cover. She took the whole bunch with her, running toward, then past the horses while showing me a mass of waving white flags. The horses didn't even look up.

I wasn't really upset. The stalk had worked, and those deer were a long way from a road. I'd been having as much fun hunting these deer with my range and equipment constraints as hunting bucks with my scoped .280.

It was still daylight, and deer were moving. It wasn't over yet, but it was beginning to feel that way, so I headed down the mountain. Cutting the distance to drag a deer if I got one, and getting closer to the truck by nightfall if I didn't.

I was nearly to the only road in the valley bottom when I saw a lone doe approaching a field dotted with two rows of round bales. When she passed out of sight behind the first row, I scampered across the farm road then hunkered down in a grassy ditch with my elbows on the flat edge of the hayfield. If she continued the way she was going, her path would soon bring her into the open at the end of the row of bales, in range, to my left.

Finally, just as I'd hoped, I was close, I had a solid rest, the sun was at my back, above the hilltops, the field before me lit like a Broadway stage. Just how it was supposed to be.

I waited, then waited some more. What happened? Did she stop? Had she gone back up the other side of the valley while obscured by the bales? I started to get up, intending to sneak to the closest bale to see where she'd gone. I'd barely gotten to my feet when I caught a flash of movement. An ear flicked once, then disappeared, right at the end of the row where I expected her to step out.

I collapsed like a marionette with severed strings, dropping back into my ditch, and waited. The sun was still above the ridgeline behind me but time, and my resolve to stay still, were both fading fast. Then, there she was, out in the open. She had retraced her steps and was now off to my right. My carefully laid out spot and rest were perfectly set up to shoot the other direction. How I squirmed and twisted in the tall ditch grass, scootching into a new position without getting caught, I can't explain, but I did it.

In the waning daylight of the last afternoon of my second year in the effort, it came together.

A perfect lung shot would have resulted in a short track, but my shot was a little high. She dropped without taking a step.

I slid another round into the chamber, reengaged the safety, retrieved my empty, then walked over. She never moved.

She was beautiful. Big for a doe, probably several years old. I gave her the last bite, called Ri to gather the crew to join me, then sat with her while the shadows continued their climb up the hillside I'd been facing when I took the shot.

Field dressing could wait. I wanted the guys to be immersed in the tableau—to see as well as hear how it played out.

Finally, with a knife that was older than the rifle, one Dad had been issued on his aforementioned cruise, I prepared my first doe in a long time, for transport.

I didn't hoist an Old Fashioned in her honor that evening, but I did last night, in a Hibachi restaurant nine hundred miles west of that hayfield.

I'm usually a gin drinker, but that Old Fashioned was pretty good. I might want to have another sometime.

Out West Quail

Though both had died before I was old enough to shave, Nash Buckingham introduced me to quail, and Robert Ruark made them my friends.

Quail, or "birds" as they were called in the literature of my youth (as in "we're going bird hunting"), were bobwhites. They were respectable. Small, feathered ladies and gentlemen who lived in the same places for generations. They were the quarry of choice for men who wore knickers, shooting jackets, even ties while hunting. In my magazine- and book-fueled imagination, after a day of pursuing these classy birds, hunters and dogs would retire to the drawing rooms of houses that had withstood the carnage of the civil war. Their stockinged feet toward a fire, the men would puff their pipes and sip smoky smelling brown liquids.

Tobacco, dogs, and Hoppes #9 would almost, but not quite, eclipse the underlying scent of aged Kentucky bourbon.

English setters with slumping eyelids would lay their big, tired heads on the legs of these men, or across their feet after a particularly long day, while the conversation would range from hunting dogs, to literature, to the news of the day.

The combination of hunting and elegance seemed to me a very grown-up contrast to my buddies and me and our dogless, BB gun pursuit of Starlings and English Sparrows.

As it turned out, my first hunting dog was a redbone plott cross. Rather than the decorous world of the quail hunter, I pledged the frat house of hound men. Our dogs were loud and rambunctious, like us. We didn't have, or want, meerschaum pipes or aged bourbon; we thrived on adrenaline, hullabaloo, and Mountain Dew. On a good night, we'd wind up wading, hip deep, in a roaring current of baying Walkers, Blueticks, and Black and Tans, while shining a six-cell Dynalite up a fir, seeking that quick glimpse of eyeshine to verify it was the right tree. Then we'd tie the dogs and flip a coin to see who would climb to wrestle the coon out for a second chase.

Hunting with hounds was noisy, politically incorrect, even in the 1970s, and glorious. Eventually it began to feel incompatible with my life as I assumed the role of husband, father, and mortgaged homeowner.

I was ready to become a, comparatively, solid citizen. I would be a bird hunter.

I understood that mule drawn wagons and bobwhites lived on the opposite corner of the country from me, so I pictured myself strolling through vast grasslands under blue skies collecting long tailed, psychedelically fledged pheasants.

I did some of that. It was fun, but it was tough finding places to hunt. The best pheasant cover was frequently leased and nearly always posted.

To avoid knocking on doors or joining one of the clubs that leased ag land, I turned to sharper featured landscape.

That's when I discovered quail, western style.

These guys shared their home with chukars and huns, as well as rattlesnakes, wild horses, and bighorns. I've had many days of chukar hunting that went from no birds to memorable outings when, in the brushy draws between chukar hillsides, quail filled in for the headliners.

Those refined English Setter men whose writing compelled me along this bird dog path would not recognize scrub country Valley Quail or desert Gambles as the same sort of bird they loved. And my whiskered Fouseks look nothing like the flag tail dogs that accompanied those hunters.

Despite their small stature and cute little topknots, these tough westerners are ornery little cusses with the power to lure us, hunters and dogs alike, into sketchy situations only to buzz away in a noisy, confusing flurry of gray projectiles exploding in different directions.

In many years of chasing quail in Washington, Idaho, and occasionally Arizona, I've never seen a buckboard, a bird hunter on horseback, or a bobwhite. I've never stayed in a lodge with an in-house chef. I have, however, broken parts of my trucks on ugly two tracks, flushed a covey from the shade of an abandoned, bullet-riddled school bus, stumbled onto a drug smuggler's roughed out cactus-lined airstrip, and frequently enjoyed gas station burritos for dinner, and breakfast.

Decades and multiple bird dogs later, other than a lack of tree climbing, I don't feel too far removed from my hound man roots.

Western quail hunting isn't always rough. I have heard tales of Northern California quail that live in rolling grasslands. A friend who winters in Arizona tells of hunting Mearns quail in wide open oak country. That sounds nice. One day, I intend to see those gentle slopes and hunt those affable quail.

For now, though, I'll stick to my badlands outlaw birds.

Whether Valley quail near my home in the northwest or Gambles in the hills of Arizona, quail hunting includes thorns. In addition to being sure to pack your vest pockets with more shells than you think you'll need, always save room for several band aids.

Surprisingly, southwestern cactus may be easier to deal with than northwestern Russian Olive.

I wonder where the quail I chase hung out before some homesick immigrant planted the first Russian Olive. Even when the birds hunker down in sagebrush, patches of that spiny olive are lurking nearby, waiting to skewer arms and faces and to snatch hats.

Thorns and the confounding way the branches entwine create tough choices.

Quail hunters learn, some more quickly and with fewer lessons than others, to pick their shots. After hearing but not seeing several flushes, it's hard to hold your fire when a quail offers an unobstructed shot. It's harder still to retrieve a tiny bird that may be on the ground but just as likely is hanging eight feet up in a claustrophobic tangle of inch-long daggers.

It's better to watch them fly then regroup in more forgiving cover.

Being occasionally impaled is part of the game. So is meeting the neighbors.

Plants aren't the only prickly things you'll find while quail hunting. My dogs have all pointed plenty of porcupines. Usually, a scolding from me is the worst of it. A few times a cluster of relatively easily removed nose quills added to the lesson. It's not always that easy, though. My dog Clancy once tried to eat a porcupine. At least that's what Jack and I concluded. Clance came out of a brushy draw looking like a department store Santa—hundreds of the white back-end of quills bristling from his face like a beard.

It was a long way to a vet, and I worried about him making things worse, so Jack manned the pliers and hemostat while I laid across Clancy fighting to control his thrashing head enough for Jack to grip those vile and tenacious prongs. It was a long, sweaty, and dusty job. Hard on all three of us. But we finished in time to get into a couple coveys before dark.

I've only hunted Arizona in January. Snakes are mostly dormant by then. At least I've not seen any. One winter morning, a Phoenix friend and I were less than a half mile from the truck when he told me he'd walked that same path on the October quail opener but turned back when he saw his eighth rattlesnake of the day.

It takes years of hard hunting and a dose of bad luck to see that many rattlers in Washington. My friend lasted about six snakes more than I would have, but he doesn't have a dog.

Having a snakebit dog once, I never want to see it again. Clancy survived, he was hunting a week later, but his pain and swelling were dramatic and frightening.

I was focused on chukars the day my dog Bogan pointed a cougar. I was confident the brush patch Bog pointed held quail. It was…stimulating when a cougar rather than birds flushed. No harm done to us or the cat, or chukars for that matter. We did get some non-cougar points and a few quail later that day.

Though rarely seen, rattlesnakes and cougars are animals we all know inhabit quail country. I never considered wild horses to be a problem, until they were. They are big, fast, and apparently don't like dogs.

Mustangs are beautiful when pacing my truck—at a distance. Up close, they're scarred, dirty, exude bad attitude, and the ground shakes when several are chasing a dog. My dogs, when intimidated, head to me for help. A dog approaching at top speed a few steps ahead of a herd of hepped up horses is an impressive sight, especially when closing fast. So far, the horses have always turned away before any of us got trampled, but they sure know how to make a point.

Injuries—and moments of lively encounters with fanged, quilled, or hoofed locals—are a spicy but ultimately uncommon part of quail hunting.

Generous limits and a willingness to hold better than their bigger, flashier, upland counterparts make quail a favorite.

Periodically Hank, an old friend, invites me to join him on private land where the quail are abundant and the cover more forgiving than usual. One spot in particular is remarkably gentle for quail cover, and a consistent producer.

It is a just right combination of water, vegetation, and slope. It also includes some standard Eastern Washington attributes. An old combine rusts away and tilts a little more each year in the small, open, grassy spot between Russian Olives and sage brush. Segments of culvert lay scattered like a spilled bowl of bar room pretzels, and parts of the brush are impenetrable.

Despite decaying metal and thorns, I find it beautiful. It is the quail spot of dreams. The swale, with a soggy center, runs east west for roughly a half mile. The west end slopes up to a, by quail season, harvested wheat field of six-inch stubble. East is the farm equipment graveyard. The thicket between, dense and prickly as it is, isn't wide enough for quail to feel comfortable holding there when we and our dogs encroach. They fly. Usually, the only bloodshed on the initial flush is from the long thorns of Russian Olive etching warnings on our faces and hands as we probe the edges. Often our only contact is to hear the quail go.

They invariably fly to the south. That's their mistake. Sagebrush hillsides aren't as picturesque as pine dotted Mearns country or gentle grasslands, but a covey of ten sprinkled over a basketball court-size patch of that pungent bush might net seven or eight points on singles.

Other times a covey will rise at once, all wings and turmoil. I often respond with two extremely quick off balance and ineffective shots, then watch a second wave, even a third wave of a dozen or more, fly off while smoke curls from the open breech of my shotgun as I flail around my pocket for more shells.

On those rare occasions when I forego the frenzy, react to the actual speed of their flight, and shoot deliberately, birds tend to fall.

It took longer than it should have, but I finally learned that the hectic eruption of a covey, or even a single or pair, happens more slowly than it seems. It's partly their small size, the blur of their wings, even the sound, but the real issue is proximity.

I've never done the math to try to figure the optimum time lag before shooting, but it's long enough to take a breath and get squared away. I've fired many baseball-size patterns into vacant spots between birds by shooting too quickly.

Sometimes it all works. My dog stiffens into a classy point, I walk alongside, hesitate with my twenty at the ready, then it happens—the wonderful sound of little wings and the chaos of quail spurting at every angle. As I touch the trigger, I clearly see a topknot and the pattern of the breast feathers, then swing to complete a double while noting the feathers floating above my first bird.

I've still never seen a wild bobwhite. My torn brush pants and faded orange vest are a long way from tweed knickers and a jacket, but I feel a kinship with the authors I read as a boy and gratitude that they introduced me to quail.

Dreamember

"I saw old Arch this morning," I said. "Haven't seen him in a long time. He's a good one, that Arch."

I was smiling at the memory. Archie was my first bird dog; if he hadn't been so good, I might have spent more time bowhunting, but he was that good. It was because of him that I followed dogs that looked a lot like him for, well I don't know how long, but there were…hell, had to be a half dozen of 'em after Arch.

I looked at my guest. How long had he been here? My smile wasn't being returned. He looked sad. Not his fault I suppose—kids in college, work, but he does seem to be a grumpy old fart. Ha, he is old. Jeez, I was…must have been about thirty when he was born. Now he's got gray hair, kind of soft looking. My son is an old man…but I was hunting with Arch this morning?

"Where were you and Archie hunting?"

Smart ass kid is humoring me now, but he doesn't know. He doesn't get dreamembering. I've tried to tell him. I think he tried to understand, but I could tell he was just playing along. Hell, I didn't understand it myself, till I did.

Insincere or not, I wanted to tell him about it. "You know, we started for chukar in the breaks of the Snake, but before I knew it, we were clear up by Plentywood and oh Gawd the pheasants."

I wish I could take him with me. He's been there before, shot his first pheasant. He skipped a week of school to go. We rented a vacant house where we'd make fried egg sandwiches for breakfast and lunch, then wash down a dinner of chicken and gems with bottles of sarsaparilla at the Reserve bar. Kids in bars. I love Montana.

"That's a good spot." Finally, a real smile. He's not dreamembering, but he's getting a glimpse.

"I'd like us to do that trip again."

"Me, too, Dad." The real smile is gone.

"You remember that story about me and Steve getting charged by that mama griz I said. Well, that happened again. I don't know, today, yesterday, but it happened a couple times."

I'm looking him right in the eye, but he faded for a second, replaced by the river, and the bear, then he's back.

"The last time it happened that old sow got closer than she ever did before."

Dreamembering is the best. I've always had good recall, but I was a great-grandpa with a dead wife before I understood the power of dreams and memories mixing up with time. That's what my boy is missing, what I wish I could show him, make him see. It's right there.

I still just remember most things, but some events…they happen again, and I'm there. It starts with a memory then, like walking through a door, I'm in it. Since it's happening again, it's not always exactly the same. I don't just relive it; sometimes I can change it. Usually the events alter themselves, but now and then I can affect the outcome.

Like that griz. When the raft drifts around the bend, she sees us and, oh boy, here she comes! I can see her twin cubs.

They're standing in the shallows downstream, river left. She's running right up the shallow river. Closing fast. I'm not collecting details and memories now, I'm there, I'm here. I see her, stretching out like a giant, misshapen brown dog. I hear her front paws slap the moving surface of the river, and clearly see each drop erupting from the impact. I feel the breeze and hear the water gurgle under the raft as I slightly shift my weight to compensate for the rocking against the soft floor while the current pulls us toward the uncertain climax. I'm leaning in, then rearing back hard, pulling on the oars with everything I've got, trying to gain a few seconds before the gap between us and the griz closes.

Bear or not, it feels so good to be young and vibrant, bending the oars. I'm powerful, up for whatever comes next. Good knees, solid strong shoulders, nothing hurts. There is a mosquito on the edge of my nose. I smell the deet on my fingers as I lean down to rub the bug against my left oar hand, wondering as I do it why I bother with a mosquito while a grizzly is bearing down. The wind is blowing upstream, from her to us. She's just defending her cubs, but I'm afraid she'll be on us before she gets our scent. Things are unfolding fast, but time has shifted. Despite the speed of the bear and the river, there is time to think, exactly like the first time. I'm wondering if Steve is cool under pressure, since he's got the gun. Will someone die today? Do we kill the cubs if Steve has to shoot? If the sow doesn't pull up…then she does. On her hind legs, dead center in the river, her eyes look placid rather than hostile. Her left "arm" hangs down, but the right is cocked as though she's ready to throw a punch. Water runs along, then drips off the ends of curved, brown, fading to ivory-tipped claws. She huffs once then drops, twisting to her right, and disappears into the brush. Steve and I lock eyes as we drift across her fading wake.

He's looking at me. Again with that damn sympathetic, half-assed smile. Kid has no clue what a rush I had while he sat there wanting to be almost anywhere else. I manage a rueful grin and just shake my head.

I wish I could share this gift, skill, whatever it is. I don't know when it started. Ha, I don't know for sure what year it is, or what day, but those don't matter. My memories matter. They're who I am; they're part of why he is who he is. Now that I get to do those things again, I can tell him…I can almost show him, but when I try, I get lost, tangled in the telling. I hear what I'm saying; there's so much to tell. It's important that he knows, but…it ain't right. It's…hell…I'd be taken more seriously if I just shut up.

But then Arch locks up. It's his first point on a wild pheasant. I know now that there are two roosters. I could easily get a double, but it was so sweet the first time, I'm going to do it the same way today. I was by myself the first time, too. It's a conundrum. This is just the kind of moment I want my boy to have from me, and his from him, but bringing someone else into this moment diminishes it. Hell, there are so many good, even perfect points in time… Ha, points, that I can leave this one like it was, like it is.

Arch is facing directly into the wind. It's blowing steady and cold but not hard. The grass is thick, waist high to a tall Indian in places but mostly a bit above my knees. He banged into that wall of pheasant scent while crossing a sparse spot. The birds are in the tall grass, but Archie's in the open. I so wanted to shoot this first bird he pointed and worried it would be a hen. But I know how this is going to play out. I know the cackle, the cold prairie sun flashing on the green, the red, and especially the white ring on the rooster's neck. The first time I nearly blew it. When that second rooster got up, I lost focus, glanced away, and almost let the first one get too far out. I'm ready for him this time though: I don't flinch at all.

A handful of feathers drift almost all the way back to me on the breeze. That rooster looks so big in Archie's mouth, almost enough to tip him over. I hug him while he holds the bird. He's quivering he's so excited; hell, I'm quivering, too. It was wonderful the first time when I didn't understand what was starting that day. It's even better now.

That bear got close today; I swear I could smell her. Steve wasn't even there.

Things are different here today, too. I don't know how I got on my back in bed, seems like I was just sitting in my chair. It's not just the boy giving me that sad smile now; his wife is here, too, trying to look cheerful. I remember when their first baby was born. My wife and I didn't know what to do. We were laughing and crying. When we left the hospital, we skipped across the parking lot to my truck, looked like a couple of knuckleheads. We had a lot of fun in that truck; almost as much fun as in my car when we were teenagers.

"Hey, babe." She swam over to the dock.

I love being with her at the lake. She's so pretty and tan. As she steps from the top rung of the 2x4 ladder to the dock, she shakes her long hair to get me wet. This is better than Arch's first bird.

I dive in and feel the cool embrace of the water but turn after just a few strokes and ascend the ladder myself just as she's settling on a too small towel on the dock.

I lay down directly on the sun-warmed wood planks facing her with my chin on my hands.

"What are you thinking?" Her eyes sparkle as she asks, but it's not a real question. She knows what I'm thinking.

I don't want to share this moment with anyone else.

It's been a while since I felt the hot sun. Hunting with Arch or floating that Alaskan river are great days, but they're cold. The heat feels terrific. August sun on me and my girl dries us and the dock in minutes, then we're back in the water swimming, laughing, and waiting for sundown.

It's a quick shift from the dock to the delivery room. She still looks pretty. She's working hard though, and unlike the first time I'm not so helpless. I can move this along. In no time, we're holding our first baby, our little girl.

Without a pause, I'm rolling in the backyard lawn. I'm trying to call my wife out of the kitchen, but I'm laughing so hard and uncontrollably, face down with my arms over my head, trying to keep a determined puppy with bristly whiskers out of my ear. I can't get the words out. The summer smell of grass and puppy and the music of my kid's laughter is the best…just the best.

From there to the worst.

I can barely see a slight rise and fall in her chest, but nothing else is going on. All the kids are here. The oldest boy brought me out here to the hallway. He is holding my shoulders, gently forcing eye contact. It's the same every time. The one damn time I can't alter things is the one I can't abide.

"Dad," he says quietly. His words have long gaps between them as he tries to sound calm and reasonable. "We, we wouldn't…let one of our dogs do this…we can't let Mom."

I know he's right, but I can't do it. I let my boy tell the tiny, compassionate Pakistani doctor that she can withhold the medication that has kept my wife, my old girl, breathing for the past few hours. In minutes, she's gone.

That damn bear is relentless. Here she comes again. Steve isn't here again today, and I'm not even in the raft this time, but afoot on the riverbank with my old Howatt Hunter in my hand. This is new. Before I can get an arrow on the string, I'm back in my room. They're all here now, kids, grandkids, but here comes that bear again. I can feel the difference; she means it this time. I've got an arrow nocked; I draw without thinking. The instant my middle finger touches my anchor, I release. She's close, the arrow takes her low in the chest, just a hint of yellow fletching visible. She stumbles a little, turns sharply to her left for a step but spins right back, makes eye contact, and keeps coming.

Everything tells me to run, but with the family here, I've got to keep the bear focused on me. Oh, Gawd! My second arrow almost hit Arch. He piled into that bear at the same time as the arrow. Good boy! I should have known he'd show up when I needed him. He's got a good grip, but he's like a bug on a windshield, she didn't even slow down. For a fraction of a second, the impact of the bear hitting me took me to high school football, but then I'm on my back, partly in the water. Oh, it's cold. I'm holding on tight, both hands full of fur. Her breath is rancid. Arch is swinging from the bear's throat. He's close enough that I can hear his low growl over the splashing. Just like I'd read, I don't feel any pain from the bites, but I know they're bad. I only have to hang on for a few seconds. Both arrows were true. Her attention is all on me. It won't be long. The kids will all get away. The bear will have to settle for just me and Arch.

I hope her cubs will be okay…

About the Author

Kevin turned 16 in March, eight days after his buddy Bruce. In the intervening days, Bruce bought a tired, green, 1955 Willys Wagon in which, during that pivotal week, the boys learned, to their complete surprise, that 4-wheel drive did not eliminate the risk of getting bogged down, it did, however, allow deeper penetration into bad places before being irretrievably mired.

That magical age of 16, with its accompanying freedom, driver's license, and their first shared tow truck bill, was a revelation. The possibilities, if not available funds, were massive.

Since those days, in addition to scratching out a degree, Kevin worked as a cook at KFC, a casual longshoreman, a swing-shift off-loader in a lumber mill, a process server (long hair, torn sweatshirt, and beard helped), in the sunrise sort at UPS, as a detailer at a Fiat dealer, a Commander at U-Haul, and a real estate salesman before beginning a long and ongoing financial advisory business.

His ramblings, including many in this collection, have appeared in Gray's Sporting Journal, Bowhunter, Salmon and

Steelhead Journal, Traditional Bowhunter Magazine, Pointing Dog Journal, Strung Magazine, and Backcountry Journal.

Kevin and his wife Laurie, who is a real good sport, raised their daughter and twin sons in the house where they still live, near Puyallup, Washington. They share the space with Colt, the current in a long line of hunting dogs, lap warmers, and chief security officers, their cat Bogey, a hedonistic shrew assassin, and a yard full of song birds and squirrels that visit feeders and keep Bogey and Colt fascinated.

Acknowledgements

Limited space and my memory make it impossible to properly acknowledge all the people who have helped or encouraged me. Some intentionally, while others have inadvertently caused tiny adjustments that altered my life and left me with memories, stories, and a new, usually enhanced perspective.

Mom taught me that reading is fun. She made it seem like it was the best thing ever, and I bought in all the way.

Dad worked six long days a week but always managed a few summer evenings for us to troll a triple teaser behind a rented rowboat on a nearby lake or to cast a worm into the mysteries of Puget Sound from a riprap lined shore. He also fit in the two or three Sundays in the Octobers of my youth to let me follow him and my uncles as they almost always fruitlessly hunted blacktail deer.

Catching an occasional pan sized trout and dreaming of what became almost mythical antlers ignited something in me that is still burning.

Thanks Mom and Dad. That blend of reading, fishing, and hunting tilted me in a direction for which I'm forever grateful.

And thanks for tolerating baying coonhounds in the yard and the wide variety of roadkill in the freezer.

By the 7th grade, I had two outdoor magazine subscriptions, a library a mile-and-a-half bike ride south of me, another the same distance to the north, and three like-minded buddies: Bruce, Duncan, and Curley.

Before long, the four of us were hunting starlings with bb guns and slingshots, and trapping mountain beavers to preserve their little hides. Sharing those exciting days of discovery with my pals put us all on a path toward fun and adventure that, despite our geographic separation, continues today. I'm so glad we grew up together.

Thanks guys.

In junior high, I was easily and often distracted by a pretty 9th grader with a great smile that was occasionally aimed my way. I did my best to increase the frequency of those intriguing glances. Laurie's grin and quick wit caught me then and still holds me as fast as those Victor #1 jump traps did those hapless mountain beavers.

In the decades since, her understanding of my need to roam, and her willingness to join me on a variety of ventures (though she usually skips the kind where blizzards are imminent) or to wish me well when she chose to stay home, has given me more time than I deserve to indulge my passions.

She's also a hard-nosed grammarian and a darn good proofreader.

Thanks Laur for all good times so far and those yet ahead.

After a couple of years with just the two of us, our baby girl Megan arrived. Soon, her twin brothers Jake and Riley came on the scene. As they grew, we had great adventures. Camping, fishing, kayaking, hunting, and lying on our backs watching meteor showers. Our hearts and our camps were full, so it seemed. That turned out not to be the case. Daughters-in-law Kelsey and Sarah, son-in-law Bajz, and grandkids Avery, Finn, and Bruce have added so much we didn't even know we needed. They've made our forays to wild and fun places better than we could have imagined, with the promise of plenty more to come.

Cooking eggs over a small smokey campfire with four-year-old Megan, or watching Jake or Ri walk in on a pointed covey of quail seemed like high points that might never be surpassed, yet each succeeding year just gets better. Now the next generation is allowing me, once again, to see so many firsts through young eyes.

Thanks to all of you. Everything is secondary to you.

I have eternal gratitude to the writers who made this path I've chosen so enjoyable. There are so many. Gene Hill, Pat McManus, Robert Ruark, Jack O'Conner, Ed Zern, Ted Trueblood, Nash Buckingham, Russel Annebelle, Burton Spiller, Ernest Hemingway, George Bird Evans, and so many others. They took me to Alaska, and showed me the desert southwest before I was old enough to camp out on my own. They introduced me to exotic beasts like whitetails, mule deer, and pronghorns, all absent from the woods near my Western Washington home. With them I experienced Africa and Mexico, marlin and giraffes. First in my bedroom with a flashlight and a magazine, then later, because of their influence, in person. Some stories taught me things a boy should know, others showed me the world and exposed me to humor and emotion in literature. Special thanks to Dwight Schuh and Don Thomas. As editors they both accepted early manuscripts I submitted, then offered advice and friendship. The diverse and effective styles of these two was a profound lesson that precision of language and passion make wonderful partners on the page, and are always in style.

I feel a debt to them all that I can never repay but I hope their influence has had some beneficial effect on my storytelling as it certainly has on my life.

Along with the masters above, accidental influences have added so much.

An overheard late-night conversation in a truck stop rocked me and made me expand my definition of success.

I heard stories people only share with strangers they know they will never encounter again, and shared smiles with solitary drivers and whole families of friendly folks who long ago stopped to offer this scruffy hitchhiker a ride, even sometimes when I was carrying a shotgun.

Jack, a longbow toting stranger I met in a meadow, miles from even a dirt road. He became a great friend and as a biologist and a hunter, is someone who always has answers to my questions about habitat and wildlife.

Patient proprietors of sporting goods stores who tolerated us kids dropping our bikes out front then handling every bow in the store, looking through the books and magazines, and peppering them with endless questions.

The three girls who cried as our English 101 prof read one of my stories to the class.

Teachers from grade school through college. I learned and benefitted from our time together, and hope I wasn't too much of a hassle in class.

The owner of a lonely out of the way gas station who, when my sick truck cut my elk hunt short, offered me his nearly new car to drive the 100 plus miles to my home because he didn't have the part on hand to fix my old ailing pickup.

"Promise you'll bring it back?"

"Yes sir," I said. We shook hands and I left to return three days later for my healed truck and a bill that was probably less than it should have been.

Stephanee at Integrative Ink for her metaphoric red pencil and advice through the administrative process of getting this book completed.

Dog friendly motel operators, ranchers who allowed access, and those who didn't but suggested alternatives, and baristas who always, even before sunrise, offer a smile and a crunchy treat for my dogs.

And, inevitably all the people I've inadvertently omitted who I'll remember later individually and in bunches.

Thank you all.